SHARK$

SHARK$

INVESTIGATING THE CRIMINAL HEART
OF THE GLOBAL CITY

Conor Woodman

CONTENTS

PROLOGUE

TONY SOPRANO. WHAT a guy. For eight years the world fell in love with the titular character from the hit HBO show and his gang of ill-doing friends. My brother was so seduced that he once confessed to me that he went through a phase of dealing with stressful situations by first asking himself, 'What would Tony do?' He's a doctor.

Criminal/gangster stories are one of the most enduring and popular genres in fiction. Whether in literature or TV and film, we are fascinated by characters who engage in nefarious deeds. Increasingly, plots glorify the rise and fall of a criminal, gang, murderer or thief and dwell on their personal power struggles with rivals or the law. Fictional criminals are portrayed on the surface as materialistic, street-smart, immoral, megalomaniacal and even self-destructive, but at the same time we are asked to believe that underneath they're also able to express sensitivity and gentleness.

But is this anything like the reality?

Four years ago I began making documentary films about crime, first for the National Geographic channel and then for ITV and the BBC. In all, I've made around thirty films about criminals of all shapes and sizes all over the world. I'm talking about the thieves, the drug dealers, the kidnappers, the rapists, the conmen, the counterfeiters and the smugglers who earn their money by operating on the wrong side of the law.

I wanted to know not just who these people were but to find out what they were about. What made them tick. Does crime really pay? Do they do it for the money or is there something else that motivates them? And how does a person sleep at night when they have taken from another with seemingly little concern for their well-being? How does the real criminal stack up against the one on HBO?

I travelled between the world's greatest cities on the hunt for the latest crimes and the criminals behind them. I particularly targeted the kind of crimes that you and I, or any tourist or business traveller, could fall foul of, and I was determined always not to dwell on the petty criminals for too long but rather to follow the chain of command as high as I could.

Today it may sometimes seem as though all crime has gone 'online' and that the most dangerous criminals are lurking in our email inbox but my experiences suggested that this is far from the case. My travels all too often resulted in me coming face to face with some extremely dangerous and unpleasant individuals who very much operate in the 'real' world.

There's often an assumption that criminals are somehow less intelligent than the wider public but my experiences suggest quite the opposite. The one thing most of the criminals I've met have in common is confidence. Whether this confidence is in their talent or their guile or simply their strength, many of these people are in no doubt that they are good at what they do. But that strength of character makes for a very good interviewee. My previous book *Unfair Trade* looked at how Big Business exploits workers around the world and also how, by banging an ethical label on their products, it simultaneously fooled us all into thinking they weren't. I'm curious about rip-offs. In order to research my films and this book the way I wanted to, I had to learn to be the rip-off merchant's best friend.

If you have ever wondered about criminal behaviour too, then the chances are that you are one of the millions of people who have been a victim of a crime, or who know someone close to you who has been, because it is people like you and me that they target. These men – and they nearly are always men – seek out people like us because we have money. If you're looking for something to take away, this book could be read as a manual for how to protect yourself from them.

This was a difficult book to write. Many of the films I have made over the years about criminals were done with the help of cameramen and producers who shared the burden of the work. I have to thank them for supporting me on this journey. Films are unfortunately by nature very time-limited and often we must pick only the best soundbite to represent an individual. But I have revisited the interviews I conducted with these fascinating characters and I'm happy that here I can afford them much more time to tell their stories. In the cold light of day, the stark brutality of their words has forced me to think of them again and wonder if they are still out there. I decided to call the book *Sharks* for that is how I see them: cold-blooded, calculating, circling around, waiting for the first sign of weakness to launch an attack. I want you to know where they lurk and how to spot them. The thought that you now are reading this does at least give me some comfort. With any luck, you'll pay heed, and that makes one fewer person I need to worry about.

CHAPTER ONE

CRYSTAL CLEAR

'Happy Mardi Gras, sweetie'

LIKE MANY TOURIST towns, New Orleans, or Nawlins as the locals know it, enjoys basking in its former glory. Although during Mardi Gras it doesn't so much bask as strip off, douse itself in oil, pour a cocktail and sprawl out naked under the hot glaring sun of its former glory. During the world's largest street parade, Nawlins is a suntanned, drunken, naturist of a town.

As with most drunks, Nawlins also has a few aliases, presumably for when other towns come looking for their money. It is variously known as the Big Easy, the City that Care Forgot, the birthplace of jazz or even the most northerly city in the Caribbean. Call it what you want, there is nothing like it anywhere else in the world. The city was once the largest slave trading port on the planet, which may explain now why it has a unique demographic of 60 per cent black and 30 per cent white inhabitants.

With the bottom having finally dropped out of the slavery market, New Orleans reinvented itself as a rival for Las Vegas as the USA's number one Sin City. Tourism is now by far the city's largest industry. Despite being ravaged by Hurricane Katrina in 2005, over 10 million visitors flock here every year, over a million of whom come for one week in February to get down and dirty, real dirty.

The celebrations for Mardi Gras, or Fat Tuesday if you prefer to *parler anglais*, begin to build over a four-week period beginning on the Feast of the Epiphany. In the last week, the party reaches a crescendo when parades and floats ride along the main thoroughfare, St Charles Street to Bourbon Street, the notorious centre of the downtown district known as the French Quarter.

I've arrived in New Orleans in the middle of the chaos. It's a week before Mardi Gras and the party is beginning to warm up. The locals tell me that every night from now on will be crazier than the one before until the craziest night of them all on Fat Tuesday.

I'm pretty sure that with a million tourists in town, I'm going to find it easy to get in trouble. Which is exactly what I'm here for. I imagine the street hustlers of the south see Mardi Gras the same way lions see the great migration of the Serengeti: feeding time.

There's one line of trouble in particular that I've read about on the margins of the press. Unsurprisingly, this being Nawlins n'all, it goes by a few different names. Some call it Cajun Bingo, most know it as the Razzle

Dazzle but the details are pretty sketchy. I know that it involves high-stakes gambling and that in the last twenty-five years it's only come to light in the media once – after a bust in 2004.

Rumours have it that the game is played in kiosks along the carnival route, others have it in back rooms in the French Quarter. Some say its dealers use a rigged board on which punters place bets. Many say the rules involve dice or marbles thrown onto the board and the rules broadly follow that of an American Football game where a player rolls to gain yards. But it's in the conversion of the dice score into yards that the scam comes in: it involves deciphering an unfathomably complicated conversion chart. A good dealer can easily exploit the mental arithmetic required so as to bamboozle a player into believing he is going to win right up to the point where he loses. Punters have reportedly lost tens of thousands of dollars in a single night.

The operators of the ring, which got busted in 2004, were paying strippers and bouncers to identify drunken targets, known as marks. They were paying them to introduce potential marks to the game they were running in a back room behind a store on Bourbon Street.

After a string of complaints by victims, the Louisiana State Police and FBI began investigating the address on Bourbon Street. Undercover state troopers, posing as marks, infiltrated the game and eventually produced evidence suggesting it was being 'protected' by New Orleans police department officers.

The two perpetrators running the game were arrested and convicted. The shop owner was Mitchell Schwartz, a ninety-three-year-old serial conman and classic old-school 'wise guy', with a rap sheet that stretched back to 1930. His accomplice was Terrence 'Scotty' Border, a well-known 'carny' with fifteen aliases, five Social Security numbers and convictions in at least seven states. Scotty had grown up touring the South with his family's carnival before he settled in New Orleans.

Schwartz died on the day of sentencing having pleaded guilty. Border was sentenced to thirty-six months' probation on the federal conspiracy charge and a further eight months in prison for racketeering and illegal possession of drugs.

Four officers were suspended from duty and never returned. Efforts to track them down have all turned up nothing. One source told me that I'd never find them: 'They've left the state. You might as well write them off as dead.'

Since then there has been no coverage of the Razzle in the press or the Internet. Although rumours circulate about its continued existence.

I decide to start my search in the heart of the Quarter. It's early on Friday morning the weekend before Mardi Gras but already the bars along Bourbon Street are pumping out music and cocktails. The hand grenade is the drink of choice here. It's so called because it's served in a green grenade-shaped cup. Although I suspect the real reason for the name is the effect it has inside your brain after you've drunk one. The exact ingredients are a closely guarded secret, which lends itself to accusations that it's made from petrol and napalm. They say a 'good one' should be served over ice, taste of melon and contain gin, rum and vodka. Either way, the sight of so many of them at this time of the morning is beginning to turn my stomach a little.

Just off Bourbon is Jackson Square; a pedestrianised area perched on the edge of the Quarter, just a stone's throw from the Mississippi. The cobbled paving stones around its north side line a busy thoroughfare for tourists, the perfect spot for street hustlers to pick off their prey. I'm on the lookout for an 'in' with some of the sketchier folk in town and I suspect some of the best connections come from those who peddle their scams out in the open. The street hustlers on Jackson Square immediately catch my eye – they are practitioners of the dark arts.

I make my way along the black railings that separate the gardens from the path, checking out the colourful signs that display the names of the individuals sat behind them. Some of their names are as colourful as the signs: Madame Clara, Zorba the Gypsy, Mistress

Mariam. Each one seems to look up mysteriously as I pass by while drawing me in with a variety of offers. 'Hey, Handsome,' says Mariam as I look down her list of services: tarot, palm, aura and even crystal ball. 'Care for a reading?'

I take a seat opposite her at a small camping table. On top of the tie-dyed purple tablecloth there are several packs of tarot cards, a variety of different coloured crystals and a large crystal ball. Mariam is an unusual-looking woman. She has all the elements needed to be conventionally pretty – large blue eyes, thick long dark hair, and an exotic olive complexion – and yet, she is not pretty. Her eyes are shrouded by a heavy monobrow, her teeth have rotted away in a manner that suggests she may have an unhealthy appetite for methyl ampheta-mine and under the tan are pockmarks in her skin that betray a less than salubrious past. When she addresses me, I notice that Mariam speaks with a distinct lisp, which sounds like the rasp of a snake.

She runs through the sales pitch, pointing out all the ways in which she can gaze into my future. I decide to plump for a tarot reading. An old roommate of mine at college used to read tarot as a bit of a party trick and I always quite enjoyed the showmanship of the display. 'Pick a deck,' she says, laying out the various creepy-looking sets of cards in front of me. 'The cards you pick are very important. Go with your instinct.'

Mariam begins to deal the cards I've chosen into four quadrants. She explains they describe past love, present love, future love and future life. I don't need a fortune-teller to tell me my past love life is a disaster area and my present one isn't looking much better. Anyone could see from the lack of a wedding ring on my finger that I'm at best unmarried, at worst divorced. But it's when she reaches the point of describing my future that I sit up and listen.

Mariam sees a strong woman in my future. She is the woman I will marry. Can she tell me anything about her? 'She has a successful career,' says Mariam. 'And children, she already has children.'

Wow, that's a really specific prediction. I used to go out with a woman who had children and it was such a car crash that I vowed never to attempt anything like it again. But Mariam has channelled the power of the occult and she seems pretty certain of it. Furthermore, she says I'm going to live to ninety, have two kids of my own and make enough but not a lot of money. I'll take that. Mariam's made me feel pretty good about my future and I'm happy to hand over the twenty-five dollars she asks for. Actually, she asked for a donation of between twenty-five and a hundred dollars, which means twenty-five in my book. But presumably she already knew that.

Next up is Zorba, who explains to me that he is fifth-generation gypsy and then warns me that the married woman with whom I am having an affair (I'm not) is trouble. Zorba seems genuinely concerned for me while he explains that this woman's husband can do me some serious harm if he finds out about us. He then predicts that I'll live to over a hundred years old and have three children. He must be confident that I'll take his advice and avoid the jealous husband.

Two more readings with New Orleans's tarot community give me life up to eighty and then eighty-five, no children and then four children, a long and happy marriage and then two divorces. By the time I finish, I'm beginning to realise that every now and again I do hear things that ring a little true. A little selective listening and you could believe whatever you wanted to.

I hear from three different readers that I am destined to do a lot of travelling in the near future, a couple tell me that my family is unsettled by the illness of a close family member (also true) and all of them are certain that I am going to be very busy with work over the next twelve months, which as I look at my upcoming work schedule right now can be corroborated in clear black and white.

Couldn't all of these 'predictions' just as easily be astute observations? I have an English accent and am therefore a traveller. It's not a stretch to guess that I might be travelling again before too long. The fact that I'm travelling and the way I'm dressed might give away that I am not poor. Add to that my age and that I'm not married and you could deduce that I might be busy with work. The sick relative I struggle a little more to find explanation for, but maybe it's a calculated percentage guess. Maybe most of us have a sick relative somewhere at any particular time.

As I'm handing over another twenty-five dollars, I'm suddenly grabbed from behind. A strong firm grasp. An unknown hand has taken hold of my shoulder and is pulling me away. My first reaction is that I'm being attacked so I struggle to try to move away but the grip is so tight that I can do nothing to stop myself being dragged around the corner. Once I stop struggling and allow myself to find my feet, I find that I'm standing opposite a man aged perhaps fifty with a tinge of grey in his hair. He is shorter than me and as he turns to face me, I am struck by the state of his nose. It has obviously been broken several times and has a huge scar that looks like it was split open and then stitched back together using a needle and twine – and probably by himself without the use of a mirror. This guy is a fighter and he is angry.

We are now alone, out of sight of the tarot readers and other tourists. He begins to interrogate me as to why I have had four readings in the space of an hour. Nobody does that, he points out. I must have a reason. Who am I? he demands. I evaluate the situation. Despite being twenty years older than me, this guy looks like he could easily kill me. He's been watching me and there's no denying that I've already blown my cover. I can't think of any reason to lie to him so I gamble that I may flush something out by coming clean.

I reveal to him why I'm here – I'm in Nawlins for Mardi Gras and I'm investigating some of the scams and hustles that visitors might fall prey to while they're in town. The man's eyes narrow as he takes it all in. Then his face transforms from anger to curiosity, back to anger and eventually settles on outright rage. He lurches forward to grab me again but I step back. He continues to come towards me shouting the whole time while I continue to back away. 'This is my sandpit.' He spits at me. 'You little monkey. You don't piss in my sandpit. Understand?' This is not going according to plan. I open my arms wide and plaintively explain that I mean him no harm, I'm not with the police, I only want to talk. I pull out all the big guns from my charm arsenal but to no avail. It's time to cut my losses and retreat to safety. I hurry my pace and walk away. Eventually he stops following.

Later that evening I'm out for a walk and decide to try my luck again. There's a guy standing on the corner of Jackson and Decatur in a top hat and tails. He's spinning a coin through his fingers and in front of him is the telltale magician's collapsible green felt table. Up close, I can see he has one blue and one brown eye. As if he was ever going to take up any other career.

We exchange the usual 'where are you from's and 'is this your first time's that form part of the hustler vernacular. I give all the right answers to reassure him that I'm an ordinary Joe just begging to be taken for a ride, which seems to work because he cranks up the routine and begins to spin my head around like a whirling dervish with a few coin tricks. Before I know it, the coin is coming out of every orifice and the magician is grinning like a cat with a mouse that has given up trying to get away.

I'm happy that he's having fun but something tells me that this magician has a few more tricks up his sleeve so I ask him if it isn't time we made this a little 'interesting'? His smile drops instantly and his eyes begin to scan nervously up and down the street before he returns his gaze and fixes it again on mine. 'I don't know what you're talking about,' he says, calm again, forcing the smile back up onto his face. He's going to make me beg?

'Okay,' I say. 'Let's play some cards.'

Most street magicians the world over have a version of the Three-Card Monte. Many use cards in a game called Find the Queen, others use matchstick boxes and a ball and call it Find the Pea, but the premise is the same: three choices, pick the right one and you win double your stake, pick either of the other two and you lose. In the right hands, you always lose.

The magician produces a deck of cards from stage left and with a deft hand he fans the pack out before selecting a queen and two numbered cards. He flips them face up onto the felt for my benefit. He then turns them over again and then slowly but surely he begins to switch them over and over. He's not doing it particularly quickly, quickly enough to make me pay attention but not so quick as to lose me. With a final flourish he drops the last card down. It should be easy to pick out the queen. All things being equal, the two numbered cards are on the outside. I pull out ten dollars from my wallet and drop it on the middle card. Of course I'm not surprised when he reveals I've selected badly – Six of Clubs. The queen is on his left-hand side. But I am surprised when he hands me back my ten dollars. 'A demonstration only,' he says firmly.

Any man who gives back his ill-gotten gains is a man I instantly trust. It doesn't happen to me very often. The magician and I introduce ourselves. Xan tells me he has been working the streets of Nawlins for several years. Before that, that he was a dealer at the casino and sometimes even moonlighted at private games for high-rollers blowing through town. The organisers of those games would often enlist magic men to deal the cards in a way that, let's say, 'favoured' the house. 'Things got pretty heavy there,' he says. That's why he went back to the street – safer. Safer than ending up in the river anyhow.

This is exactly the kind of break I've been looking for. A way into the higher-stakes stuff and possibly even the Razzle. I ask Xan if he's ever heard of the Razzle Dazzle. But then everything changes.

Xan begins to fold up his table quickly. He's shaking his head and he's broken off all eye contact. 'Man,' he says in a deflated voice like I've just claimed to be the father of his kids. 'You don't even want to be asking about that around here. That's just bad news.'

I place my hand on the table to try to stop him leaving. 'Just one more game,' I implore. 'Then I promise I'll leave and you won't see me again.'

Xan shakes his head again and places his upturned top hat on the table while he rubs his ruffled brow. He looks at me quizzically as if to ask 'Why am I helping you?' I drop a folded fifty-dollar note into the hat to help him out with that. 'A demonstration only,' I say. He leaves the fifty in the hat and replaces it on his head. He begins to talk again as he shuffles the cards and asks me to take one and look at it. I do that. Ace of Clubs.

'Listen,' he says, 'I like you but you gotta know that game's bad news. I heard stories about guys having guns put to their heads until they play long enough to lose and worse.'

'What could be worse?'

'Nobody knows how many people are buried in that river, my friend. Take my advice: find another game.'

And with that, Xan shakes my hand, folds the table under his arm and disappears into the shadows of Jackson Square. I head back towards Bourbon Street to get a drink. It's been a long day, I've found some evidence that the Razzle still exists but I'm no closer to tracking down an actual game and besides, I've got nothing but sick relatives and stepchildren to look forward to when I get home.

As I'm walking back towards the Quarter, I reach into my pocket for my phone to check my messages. But the phone isn't the only thing that comes out of my pocket. Fluttering down to the ground is a blue playing card. I pick it up and turn it over – it's the Ace of Clubs and written across it are the words: 'Blue Note Bar. Tomorrow. 7p.m.'

The Blue Note Bar is a two-room dive just fifty yards off the main drag, which is far enough to mean it's quiet. When I arrive there's a couple of waifs and strays at the bar who look like they've come for a few minutes' respite from the relentless revelry of the Mardi Gras. I order a rum and lime and take a seat. This feels weird. I've been on a couple of blind dates in my life but never set up by a magician.

A tall gangly-looking sort of guy comes and sits next to me at the bar. He's dressed up for the party in a bright blue top hat and red and white striped tails. He's a regular Uncle Sam. He orders whiskey, loudly, and gets into a conversation with the girl next to him about some ball that's going on across town. I'm so distracted by it that I almost don't notice the stool next to me is taken by another girl. By the look of her, she's alone.

I introduce myself and she tells me her name is Mel. She's an attractive woman, mid-to-late twenties with a tumble of dark curls that match her eyes. I offer to buy her a drink and she asks the bartender for a gin and tonic and two shots of tequila which have barely hit the back of our throats when she asks him to line up another two. That's five drinks. In less than two minutes.

The bar has two large windows that open out directly on to the street. They're framed by wooden shutters that I guess are typical of most of the buildings in the old French Quarter. It's a pleasantly warm evening and Mel and I are on the stools nearest to them. Our conversation flows easily until it is interrupted by the unmistakable sound of gunshots and then the commotion of a crowd on the move. Outside the window, on the street below, people are running, actually fleeing Bourbon Street.

The French Quarter attracts all kinds of lowlife during the Mardi Gras. People from all over the state and beyond come here with one purpose: to get plastered. It's an important ingredient in the chaos that ensues. Add into that mix the USA's penchant for guns and you have a recipe for disaster. Tonight is a case in point. Mel leans out of the window, her G&T lolling in her right hand while her left points at a young black man standing on the pavement looking back up the street. 'What's happening, sweetheart?' She's like something out of an old movie. He explains to her that when he heard shots he started running and that the cops were in there pretty *tout suite*. I suggest we go take a look but Mel's not interested. 'Someone got shot,' she says so matter of factly I wonder if she's even listening to herself. 'What you gonna see? Either a dead person or a nearly dead person. Ain't no fun in that.'

I order another couple of drinks. With a polite dip of the head, Mel takes her reloaded G&T and excuses herself for the ladies' room. I sit and wonder if we shouldn't take a walk anyhow, just for a change of scene. It doesn't look as though my date is going to show. It's already gone 8 p.m.

It's 8.10 p.m. when I realise Mel's not coming back.

Uncle Sam turns his attention around to me. 'You been hustled, my friend.' He purses his lips together as though the words tasted unpleasant to say. 'I'm sorry to tell you but this is an old trick during Mardi Gras. How many drinks you buy her anyway?'

'Four,' I tell him.

'Wow. She did well out of you for an hour's work.'

I can't disagree. I've been charmed out of around twenty-five bucks' worth of liquor by a woman I'll likely never see again. And no doubt she's on to the next Joe at the next bar somewhere further along Bourbon while I'm left talking to a guy who looks like he just walked out of a cartoon.

My new drinking buddy's name is Chris and he says he grew up right here in Nawlins, which makes him a rare thing in this town during Mardi Gras: a genuine local. I begin to tell him exactly how much fun I'm having. Starting with my adventures in fortune-telling.

'Oh, you met Gypsy John?' he drawls at me. 'He ain't nothing to be frightened of. Well, he is but you just gotta know how to handle him right. What you wanna know from him anyway?'

Next morning, I'm walking back along the southern shore of the Mississippi River, which now gives me the creeps since I know how many corpses are in it. Uncle Sam has set me up another meeting with the guy he calls Gypsy John. The guy who was running the tarot-card outfits over on Jackson Square. Chris says the guy's calmed down enough to meet me.

I'm trying to work out whether to blame the rum or the tequila for the headache that's squeezed its way uncomfortably between my ears. I'd have stayed in bed had Chris not insisted that I meet John as soon as possible.

Right off the bat I can tell this isn't going to be easy. John's waiting for me, dressed in a smart brown suit with sunglasses that make him look as intimidating as he was last time we met. My offer of a handshake is greeted with only a disdainful glance away and then without missing a beat, he asks me who the hell I am.

After a few minutes of cooking up my best charm and apology recipe, he begins to soften. I explain to him that I wasn't looking to cause trouble but the tarot readers seemed like a good place to start on the hunt for information in the city. Chris mustn't have filled him in on too many details because he's listening intently, nodding the whole time. Finally, I come to the punch. I want in on a game of Razzle. And ... nothing. He's the first person I've said that word to in town that hasn't either blanched or run a mile in the opposite direction. He simply nods silently and then, 'Maybe I can help you with that. But what's in it for me?'

The question was clearly meant to be rhetorical because John doesn't wait for me to offer. He already knows what's in it for him. He doesn't want money because instead he has a job for me. 'You scratch my back and maybe I'll scratch yours,' he says. We walk and talk while he explains to me that he's caught in the middle of a long-running family dispute that's in danger of getting nasty. But John has a game plan that requires a player with my kind of skills. He wants me to go undercover for him.

Tarot in Nawlins has been controlled by John's family

for six generations. The family originated from Romania via New York and settled in Louisiana more than fifty years ago. John's extended family of cousins and in-laws are variously involved in a carefully coordinated industry of fortune-telling. John admits openly that there's good ones and bad ones. Most of the bad ones are harmless but some of them are becoming bad for business. And he means one in particular.

On the outskirts of town, we take my hire car through suburbs that most tourists only see from the highway. Small billboards and signs along the route advertise New Orleans' delights: casinos, massages and motels. There are even a couple offering tarot and aura readings. John says these are for his cousin's business. She's a clairvoyant who runs her operations from a house on the side of the main road.

'She's become a problem,' says John in his slow Louisianan drawl. 'I already moved her out of town but it's time she left the state.'

I wonder whether this isn't a euphemism for something far more sinister. His plan is that I will help him to hasten that process by visiting her for a consultation with a concealed recording device. John's convinced that she will attempt to extort a large sum of cash from me and he wants to record the evidence so that he can use it as proof when he appeals to the other senior members of the family to sign her exit visa.

He wants me to wear a wire into a gypsy's house.

I make a call to the number on the billboard and arrange a consultation for ten minutes' time. Just enough time to drop John a safe distance away in a fast-food car park and turn back round to make my appointment. There are five other cars in the driveway when I arrive. Two wild-looking young men in their mid-twenties eye me with suspicion as I park the car in the last remaining spot. I dare say they wouldn't be happy if they knew my real reason for being here. I can hear duelling banjos playing in my head as I walk past them to the door.

I knock at the door of a lean-to structure attached to the side of a single-storey building. A rotund dark-haired woman in her mid-forties, who introduces herself as Grace, asks me in. 'You Conor?' she asks. 'Take a seat, Conor.' I think to myself that her repeating my name is probably a trick of the trade. She ushers me behind a screen where there's a metal-legged office-style table and two chairs and we sit opposite each other while she runs through the options. Thirty dollars for a basic reading. Sure. That sounds fine. I encourage her to start and she begins dealing out the cards.

There's nothing unusual about the reading. Same old clichés that I heard before. I'll travel. I'll meet someone. Life will be hard. Life will be good. I can't see anything more wrong about this than I can John's business. She asks me about my love life and I repeat the brief that

John gave me coming in. 'I've recently become estranged from my girlfriend,' I lie. 'But I'd love to get back with her.'

This is the touch paper that was waiting to be lit. She moves effortlessly into another gear. The next cards tell her that I am up against a ticking clock. Not only has my girlfriend begun seeing someone else, but I can only stop that relationship and get my own back on track if I begin an immediate course of treatments that involves me spending thousands of dollars. I'll need a candle that will cost over a thousand dollars alone, plus several more hours of her time to administer it. She assures me in her calm soothing voice that this is my only hope.

I try to imagine what I'd do if I was genuinely in this situation and at all vulnerable. I'd be under enormous pressure to open my chequebook. I understand why John has decided this woman isn't helping the family reputation. I place my hand on the recorder in my pocket and check it is still recording. It feels warm. Good. I'm happy that I've got what I came for so I decide to make my excuses and get the hell out before someone gets suspicious and discovers the wire. I thank Madame Grace. 'I'll think about the candle,' I say and hand her thirty dollars as I leave. She forces a smile like a bulldog stifling a growl.

Avoiding eye contact with the *Deliverance* twins, I slowly back the car up and pull out onto the highway.

When I reach the place where I left John, I can breathe again. He's been listening on the headphones and judging by his face, he's happy with what I've got. I guess I've made a friend. Maybe a friend who can hook me up with a game of Razzle.

The Mardi Gras has been building slowly over the last two weeks but tonight it hits top gear. The main floats are making their way into the downtown areas and many of the streets are blocked off so that revellers can line the route and collect the millions of beads being thrown at them as they pass. I'm heading back to the French Quarter looking for a girl that John has told me might be able to help me find a Razzle game. He says she's a fixer and her name is … well let's call her Crystal.

I'm heading down Bourbon Street again, slowly becoming immune to its charms. Neither the boobs nor the beads seem to have any allure for me any more, if they ever did. I want to get myself into a Razzle game and then get out of this place. But to do that I need to first find Crystal. The description I have doesn't exactly fill me with confidence. John told me that she'll be the naked girl posing for pictures outside the 5X bar just over halfway down the main drag. Not 'a' naked girl. 'The' naked girl. In this town, that doesn't seem to narrow it down enough but it's my best shot. As I approach 5X I can hear a crowd making a ruckus.

I push my way through people straining their necks to watch the entertainment happening inside the scrum. Eventually I get a clear view of the main attraction; a girl, maybe five foot four, painted silver from head to toe and wearing nothing but a silver G-string. She's posing for pictures with drunk guys. The guys must feel that ten dollars buys them an access-all-areas pass because they're putting their hands where their wives probably wouldn't want them to. Crystal's smile is permanently fixed to her face, probably quietly thinking to herself about how all those pictures will be nervously deleted in the morning while directing every note to a small wooden box nestled between her feet.

I'm mesmerised for a few moments by the seemingly endless stream of lechers taking turns on the naked silver girl. Then I snap out of it and remember John's instructions. He said that if I put a crisp hundred-dollar bill in her box, Crystal will grant me a personal audience and I can ask her about the Razzle. It seems unlikely but if nothing else it might put a stop to this grope-fest that I'm watching, which is worth a hundred dollars. I push my way forward and slide the hundred into the box so she can clearly see it. I have to shout a little to be heard over the din: 'A friend tells me that for a hundred dollars you can help me find something I'm looking for.' Her smile drops and suddenly I can see her real face. She eyeballs me straight, bends down, picks up the box and with a sharp look says 'Follow me', then turns tail and disappears into the crowd. This is my kind of girl.

'So what is it you're looking for, sweetie?' she asks as she walks ten to the dozen around the corner and up a side street heading away from the party. 'Drugs? Girls? What? Come on, I don't have all night.'

I'm a little startled at how surreal the situation has become. I'm chasing a naked silver pixie through the country's largest street party and she's offering me a shopping list of vice. When we get to the next corner she stops to unlock a bike chained to a lamppost. It gives me a second to get myself together. I don't want to spook her so I try hinting at what I'm after to see if she's happier talking around it a little.

'I want to play a game.'

'What kind of game? There's the casino right there.'

'No, I want a street game. Something local.'

'I can get you into a poker game but not to—'

I hold up my hand to interrupt her; this might have been the wrong way to go. I look down to my feet as though the right question is written on my shoes. 'No. I'm not talking about poker. I want a real local game, the kind of game they only have here in New Orleans.'

She gives me a very different look. Her eyes narrow like she's trying to work out if I'm actually going to say it or not. Of course, I am. 'Some people call it Cajun Bingo, some call it the Razzle …' There I've done it. Final roll of the dice.

Crystal mustn't be a dice player. She's taking off down the street at a pace, half running, half mounting her bike as she shouts over her shoulder. 'You don't know what you're talking about.'

I've stopped in my tracks for a moment. Hesitating. This wasn't how this was supposed to play out. Crystal is supposed to be my ticket to a game, the girl that can get you anything you want in this town. But this girl is seriously freaked and unless I chase her, this could be the end of the road. Before I know it I'm running after the naked silver pixie on a bike.

'Crystal! Crystal!' I shout after her. 'Wait!' She stops at the intersection and I catch her up. 'What's the problem?'

'That shit doesn't even exist,' she says with a sharp intake of breath.

'But I heard—' I don't get to finish my sentence because she starts talking again.

'You heard what? Shit you read on the Internet? You don't know what you're getting into. You don't have enough money anyhow.'

Hang on a minute. That doesn't make sense. 'Either it doesn't exist or I don't have enough money. Can't be both. Which is it Crystal?'

She looks at me again. This look I can't read. It could be her sizing me up or it could be her calculating what it's going to cost. Maybe a bit of both. She smiles, at least I think it's a smile, it's not the smile I saw her give the punters back on Bourbon, this is a subtler affair, like it's all for her. Before I can stop myself, I'm smiling a little too. YES! I think I've cracked her. Crystal starts to shake her head. 'You're gonna need a lot more money. A hundred dollars isn't enough for me to even start asking those kind of questions.'

I'm still smiling. This is a breakthrough. 'Sure. Who are you going to ask? And how much more are you going to need?'

'There's people but you're going to need to pay me up front – three hundred dollars and then you wait for me to call you. These aren't people that you can just call. I know people that might be able to call people but you're gonna have to just wait and see. Sorry, sugar, that's the best I got for you.'

There's something about her reluctance that's convincing me. Maybe she's scamming me for three hundred bucks and I'll never hear from her again but so what? She's my last chance. If I turn and walk away then my search for the Razzle is over anyway. So what's another three hundred dollars? I hand over the cash and make her plug my mobile number into her phone. And with that done, she's gone. The naked silver bike-riding pixie girl disappears into the crowd and the night. And I head to the nearest bar for a bourbon on the rocks. I have a feeling it's

going to be a long wait. Might as well enjoy it. Then she
rings. She tells me I will need one thousand dollars.

I head back to meet Crystal as arranged on the corner of
Bourbon and St Louis at 11.30 p.m. By now Bourbon is
awash with the detritus of Mardi Gras revelry: trashed
American tourists parading up and down aimlessly lost
and disgracefully proud of it. The corner is packed with
them and I'm wondering why on earth she'd choose such
a busy place to meet. Eventually I spot her on the corner
fumbling with her phone.

Crystal is still in costume. Or lack of one. Naked again
from the waist up and painted head to toe in silver body
paint. She greets me with yet another indecipherable smile.
I get a fleeting kiss on the cheek before she turns and heads
quickly down St Louis. I'm already beginning to understand that my role in this relationship is simply to follow. I
catch up with her just as she issues me a last warning. 'I'm
gonna say this one last time, sweetie. If I were you, I would
turn around and walk away, but if you're determined to do
this, then I'll take you where you need to go.'

Ever since I arrived in New Orleans my goal has been
to play the Razzle. I've asked just about every street rat
and hoodlum I've met since I got here and been deflected,
discouraged and just plain warned off. Now I can feel I'm
close, perhaps just moments away from finally finding out
the truth about the most elusive of scams and I can feel

my pulse racing. All those warnings are racing through my head in fast forward: Xan's talk of guns placed to your head and bodies washing up in the Mississippi River, Crystal's extreme reaction to the mention of the Razzle and a drunken flashback to Chris warning me to stop even asking about it. Yet, I know there is no way that I'm going to turn around now. I am following the naked silver pixie girl down a quiet street in America's murder capital to play this game, even if it kills me.

We stop abruptly at a doorway on St Louis. A tall rakish-looking man wearing a mask is loitering at the door. Ordinarily one might be concerned at the sight of a man wearing a mask in the street but this is New Orleans during Mardi Gras so I roll with it. The man and Crystal exchange a look and then he turns to unlock the door. Crystal ushers me inside to a dark corridor. The door closes behind us and we are alone in the darkness.

Gradually my eyes adjust to the light inside. At the end of the corridor is a room from which there is a dim light. A candle, maybe. It's hard to be sure but it throws enough light down the tunnel to make out Crystal's face. She whispers strongly in my ear. 'Okay, sweetie, let me see your money.' I pull out my wallet and reveal a grand in fifty-dollar bills. She seems reassured and taps the wallet to tell me to put it away. 'Follow the corridor to the room at the end. Place the money on the table and don't touch the mask.' There's a cold bluntness to her voice and I realise that this is all the instruction I'm going to get. I leave her at the door and do as she said.

I walk slowly down to the room. Inside there is a low table with two stools. On the table is a mask sitting on top of a small white cushion. A large candle provides the room's only light except for a dim glow coming from the top of a spiral staircase along the room's back wall. As I place my thousand dollars onto the table next to the mask, I am drawn again to the staircase by the sound of metal on stone. 'Dink, dink, dink.'

At first all I can make out in the gloom are the feet and then slowly I realise that the sound is being made by a baseball bat. A man wearing a hood and a large mask is coming down the stairs and on every step he pauses momentarily to tap the bat solidly off the edge of the stone. I can feel the blood rise up in my throat and I think to myself, 'I fucking hate this.'

As he comes closer to me I can make out his dark eyes behind the mask and he shoves the end of the bat to my chest. 'Sit down.' He's local. I can tell from the long southern drawl to his voice. I do as he says. 'Now, who the fuck are you?' he barks in my face.

I start to explain that my name is Conor and I've come from London but he interrupts with the same question, 'No. Who the fuck are you?' This time he sounds angrier than before. I start to repeat my answer but he interrupts with the same question again before he adds, 'We've been following you since you got here. We've seen you out in the streets. We know you've been asking questions about things you shouldn't have been asking about.'

'Like the Razzle?' I ask

'Yeah, like the Razzle. Where did you even hear about that? We ain't played that game down here for twenty years.'

I tell him about the articles I've found on the Internet, stories about busted games and corrupt police officers ending up in jail for being complicit. I tell him I know about the game that ran on Bourbon Street and that I know it wasn't twenty years ago. I've heard rumours that the game still exists. My heart is beating so hard in my chest that I can hear the blood in my ears. He begins to nod and he leans forward resting on the handle of the bat between his legs.

'So, you wanna play the Razzle.' He laughs again and looks over my shoulder past me. 'You okay, Crystal baby?'

I'd almost forgotten Crystal was there. I turn to see that she has come into the room and is now standing behind me. What is more, she now has an AK-47 assault rifle slung over her shoulder and it is firmly pointed at me. 'Yeah, I'm okay,' she says in that oh-so-sweet soft angelic southern voice of hers.

I turn back to the man in the mask. We both know that I'm not getting out of here without his say-so. 'Okay,' I say. 'Are we going to play or what?'

'Sure. You wanna play the Razzle. Be my guest.' He reaches out across the table to remove the mask that is sitting on the cushion next to the candle. As he pulls it away, I see the six-shooter pistol and next to it a single bullet. 'There's the Razzle,' he growls. 'Still wanna play?'

All the moisture in my mouth runs immediately dry. My eyes actually lose a little focus. What the hell have I gotten myself into here? I'm stuck in a dark room in the French Quarter with a gun pointed at my back and I'm being offered a game of Russian Roulette. A one-in-six shot at suicide. I came looking for a high-stakes gambling game but the stakes here are suddenly way higher than I can bear.

'You're telling me that the Razzle is a game of Russian Roulette?' I realise that I'm stating the obvious but a part of me is hanging on to the remote possibility that there's another option.

'No. The Razzle ain't that,' laughs my masked friend. 'Because you ain't gonna take this bet. You're gonna do what every other lily-assed tourist does when they play the Razzle. You're gonna get up and just walk out that door because you ain't got the balls to pick up that gun.'

He's right. Of course that's exactly what I'm going to do. I've placed my bet. The thousand dollars on the table is a stake placed. I could play. If I want to, then the odds of six to one are there for me to take but I'm not going to play. Nobody is. It's a perfect scam: a gambling game in which the house always wins, because every time the punter walks away before the game is over.

I get back to my feet, a little dizzy and nauseous. The masked man is already counting the cash I've left on the table and Crystal is waiting to show me out. 'I think it's time for you to leave, sweetie,' she says with a gentle wave of her assault rifle. I take it as a cue to go and I stumble slightly back down the corridor with Crystal walking closely behind. As she opens the door for me, she whispers sweetly again in my ear, 'Happy Mardi Gras.' And dispatches me back onto the street outside.

It's after midnight and Mardi Gras is almost over. Tomorrow will be Ash Wednesday and the start of Lent. I can see Bourbon Street is still full of drunken people partying. Any minute, the police will begin their traditional walk down the street to mark the end of the festival. Forming a cortege of officers on foot and horseback, they march the length of the road pushing people off the street. In times gone by, it was a signal to people that it was time to go home, but now it has become scornfully known as 'Screw the Blue' because the crowds simply step inside the bars for a moment, wait until the cops have passed, and then re-emerge onto the street to continue partying into the small hours. For tonight at least, law on the streets of New Orleans is only ceremonial.

CHAPTER TWO
THE ARTIST ·

'Apart from death, you can fix everything here'

ON BEHALF OF those who, like me, would rather eschew a violent existence, I thought it would be interesting to explore some of the non-violent crimes available to the would-be criminal. There are plenty of careers available to those who'd rather rely on brains over brawn, on guile over guns and these criminals fall into two camps.

In one camp, there's the cocky confidence tricksters, who are happy to get up in your face, smiling innocently like they're your best friend while simultaneously conning you out of your hard-earned dollars. More of these guys later. First I'd like to attend to the other camp, an altogether harder bunch to track down. These faceless criminals work in the shadows with the intention of never ever being seen by the likes of you and me. These guys get rich on the sly. They pull the strings, they call the tunes, they rely on other criminals to do the dirty work while they float innocently above all the nasty business of crime like superheroes. My favourite of these, and you've probably seen one in a black-and-white movie or two, is the forger.

There are many things that can be copied or ripped off for a quick profit. From DVDs to great works of art, there's a market in providing a knock-off of someone else's intellectual property for a knock-down price. Before the iTunes/Amazon/Netflix revolution, I can remember walking the grubby streets of Bangkok and Bali where DVDs of the latest Hollywood releases were on sale for a dollar. Or eight for five dollars if you wanted a deal. At the other end of the scale, I recall a 'friend of a friend' walking into my local pub one night offering for sale a brilliant copy of an LS Lowry painting for a few hundred pounds. Unbeknownst to him, it turned out to be a stolen original LS Lowry, worth a couple of hundred thousand pounds, and he spent three years in prison for handling stolen goods, but you get the idea.

I've arrived in Buenos Aires in midsummer. Christmas has just passed and I'm enjoying the January sunshine during a time when it's cold and grey back home. I'm in town to try to answer a question that's been bugging me, which is: if you're able to copy great works of art, then why don't more forgers simply miss out the middleman and copy actual money instead? The notes, the cash, the folding. This is what we're interested in after all. It's with this question in mind that I'm here in Argentina to look for one of the most notorious counterfeiters of all time. A man simply known as La Artista.

Argentina has a noble history of counterfeiters. During the days of fascism in Argentina under Isabel Peron in the mid-1970s, the counter-revolutionary underground used counterfeiting as a means of destabilising the government. The insurgents illegally reproduced millions of pesos of fake bills, known as falsos, and fed them into the mainstream circulation. The logic of the rebels was that the influx of this dirty cash would increase the money supply, which in turn would create a cycle of hyperinflation which in turn would destabilise the regime. It worked. National strikes and violent protests ensued and in 1976 Peron followed many of her fascist counterparts into exile in Spain.

With the fascists out the way, the counterfeiters were presented with a new opportunity. They had the machines and the know-how to reproduce currency to their hearts' content. So with no 'cause' to fight for any more, they simply began to put their skills to personal use. They cranked up the printing presses again and revolutionaries quickly became gangsters. But with so much at stake, there was the inevitable fight for control and alas, where there's gangs and guns, there's also death and destruction. In-fighting erupted.

But there was one key element that everyone knew was needed no matter what happened. One person that you couldn't afford to kill. It wasn't enough to control the printing presses, you also needed the guy who could operate them.

A printing press is only as good as its setter. The process of taking a design and copying it with the precision necessary to make a counterfeit bill is an extremely fiddly one. For this reason, the work is mostly done by those with a degree of artistic flare. On the streets of Buenos Aires, the variation in quality of work is as obvious to see as in an art gallery in London or New York. You only have to take a taxi ride to see for yourself.

I hail a cab in downtown BA not far from my hotel. I'm dressed like most tourists in February in a light shirt and jeans, carrying the obligatory guidebook for the city and acting as casual as I can so as not to arouse suspicion. At the corner, a cab pulls over and I hop in. I'm being driven downtown by a chubby, balding fifty-year-old guy who looks like … well he looks like cab drivers do in most of the world. I ask him to take me to Buenos Aires' most touristy area, La Boca. According to my guidebook the trip should cost around ninety pesos.

It's an unremarkable journey between my hotel and La Boca. Buenos Aires is a commercial city built along the banks of an estuary. The centre looks very European; the roads are wide and many of the bigger landmark buildings were built in the European style, which is why it is known as the 'Paris of South America'. But then everywhere can claim to be the Paris of somewhere. I wonder what the Coventry of South America looks like.

La Boca is popular with tourists mainly because its main drag, La Caminito, is a colourful pedestrianised street full of bars and restaurants where you can watch locals dance the tango and sample the man-sized steaks and Malbec red wine that Argentina is famous for. All the semi-naked Latin couples spinning around with their limbs entwined should create quite a romantic vibe but the foreigners ambling up and down the street posing for selfies and buying postcards manage to dampen it down some.

My taxi pulls up at the northern end of the Caminito where the driver reassuringly informs me the price is eighty pesos. I should be (and I am) immediately suspicious of a taxi driver charging the correct fare but for a second let's give him the benefit of the doubt. Eighty pesos is a bargain so I decide to celebrate by stopping for a coffee at a nearby cafe. It's lunchtime and the area is already bustling.

I pick a pretty little cafe with a striped awning and comfortable-looking chairs laid out along the street. I order myself a coffee and hand the guy behind the counter the twenty-peso note I just got in my change from the taxi driver. The coffee guy smiles but then he double takes on the note. He holds it up to the light and shakes his head. 'Sorry, my friend,' he says, passing me back the note. 'This is falso, a fake, it's no good.' I look at the crumpled bill. It's hard to be sure, but I swap it out and hand him another twenty-peso note from my wallet. He checks this one too. 'Yes. Better,' he says. 'This one is good.' I can have my coffee.

As I sit down, a couple of tourists who overheard the conversation come over. They're Americans, overlanding across South America and say they had a similar experience to me; taxis passing them dodgy counterfeit bills. 'They charged us more than the correct fare,' one of the Americans tells me, 'and then they gave me fake change.' Boom. Double whammy. When I tell them my own story, they say they've heard it dozens of times from tourists staying at their hostel. Sometimes they heard drivers will switch a real note for a fake one, hand back the fake as though the mistake was yours, ask you to pay again, keep the original real note and then pocket the second real note too. If you're really unlucky then the driver can finish the deceit by passing you fake change. Boom. Triple, quadruple, I've lost count, whammy.

When we are away from home, out of our comfort areas, we are vulnerable to criminals. The reasons may be twofold. First, we are seduced by the romance and relaxation of a sunny holiday destination so we don't exercise the same vigilance as we do at home. Second, time is at a premium on holiday so we are much less likely to seek retribution if we are the victim of a crime.

I sit for a while and watch the guy behind the counter dispensing coffee to more tourists. In the half an hour I'm there, he returns fake bills to a couple more customers. There's a serious racket going on here.

One thing I've learned is that if you want to find the guy at the top, then it's best to try to get in with one of the guys at the bottom first. What I need is to find a bent taxi driver who will talk.

So I devise a plan. I repeat the journey from Caminito to the hotel a handful of times. But I have a trick up my sleeve. Each time, before I get in the car, I surreptitiously take a picture with my phone of the hundred-peso bill I'm going to pay with. All my notes have come straight from the ATM, so I'm pretty sure they're legit. But if the driver switches my note, then I'll have the evidence. The first couple of taxi rides back and forth are unremarkable, but on my third, I get a bite.

This driver is another balding, slightly overweight fifty-something guy who grunts at me as I get in. He understands where I want to go and we drive in silence down the now familiar route. He's certainly not trying to rip me off by taking me the long way round because the meter is clocking up the fare at the right rate. When we get to the drop off, the cost is bang on what it was the last two times – eighty pesos – so I hand over a hundred-peso note. What he doesn't know is that I have already taken a picture of the thirteen-digit alphanumeric serial number on it, which ends with the characters 99K.

My driver takes the note and turns away as though he's looking for some change. Then a moment later he spins back round holding up the note. 'Amigo, this is falso.'

'Is it?' I say. I take the note to look more closely at it.

'Yes.' He says confidently. I check the serial number. The note that he has handed back to me ends not in 99K but in 76L. This is not my note. Caught him red-handed and I have the evidence.

I hold up the hundred pesos. 'This is not my note.'

'Yes. It is.'

I show him the picture. He doesn't realise what I'm doing so he keeps repeating that the note is a fake. He looks a bit confused when I agree. But it's not my note. When he realises what I'm accusing him of, his denial is point blank. 'No,' he says with outraged innocence. 'Yes.' I counter and I show him the photo of the serial number ending 99K. Slowly he begins to realise what has happened. He looks again at my phone and the penny drops. He's been exposed. Nowhere to run. He throws his hands up in the air with a loud cry of exasperation and outrage as though I am the one who has done something wrong. Shame on me for trying to catch him out!

'Look, buddy, I don't care about the hundred pesos. Keep it,' I tell him. 'I'm more interested in your story.

Everything is tranquilo and we don't need to involve the police.'

He nearly chokes on the word. 'The police!' he repeats. 'No, don't call the police!' He gets a bit panicky and tries to return my original note. But when I insist he keep it he looks confused.

'Keep it in return for explaining to me how the scam works,' I offer.

He takes a suspicious look around. He seems to be weighing up his options. Nothing to lose and a hundred pesos to gain. 'Keep it?'

I nod and with a shrug he puts the hundred pesos back in his wallet and begins to explain.

He picks up fake notes from a dealer downtown. He says he can get good counterfeit fifties and hundreds for half their face value. Over a good week, if he can pass off twenty to thirty bills to unsuspecting tourists, he adds over two thousand pesos (two hundred dollars) to his income. Low risk; high return. By sticking to tourists he kills two birds with one stone. A tourist is much less likely to recognise a fake note than an Argentine would, and if they do then they're much less likely to involve the police. Who wants to spend a day of their vacation hanging around the police station making reports for the sake of ten bucks?

What strikes me about this guy is how comfortable he is with what he's doing. He doesn't seem like a bad man but there's no hint of shame about what he's up to. He's got a family, kids and a wife and he's not doing anything that everyone else isn't also doing. It's funny, because now that he's revealing to me the details of the kind of conman he is, I suddenly find myself not only trusting him, but even liking him. It's as if the pretence that he has to put on to pull off the con was masking the nice guy underneath. It strikes me that for a guy like this to get involved in something so dishonest, it has to be pretty common. Common enough for him to think he's not doing anything wrong.

I tell him that I'm in the market for a few 'falsos' myself and after a bit of persuasion he agrees to call his 'dealer' for me. The guy runs a few bureaux de change kiosks in the centre of town and I'll have to go there if I want to arrange a transaction. I'm grateful to my new friend. I wish him well and decide to stay in Caminito to kill a couple of hours while I wait for the meeting with the next guy up the chain. It's been a successful morning's work.

Despite being one of Buenos Aires' top tourist attractions, the Caminito is really just three streets of cafes and restaurants in an otherwise crime-riddled area of the city. Venture more than a block from the crowds and you're asking for trouble. For lunch I order a steak that's bigger than my head and enjoy it while watching a couple of professional dancers turn a tango around the floor that's so intimate that it feels like watching a live sex show. Afterwards I take a taxi back uptown to my hotel to prepare for this evening's rendezvous.

My meeting is set for a kiosk along a busy street in the centre of town at 7 p.m. When I arrive, I spot a guy who fits the description, casually standing outside the kiosk, smoking a cigarette, next to half-a-dozen armed cops. I have a mini-panic that this is some kind of set-up. Have I been duped into falling for a sting? I know enough to know that you do not want to be the tourist who gets arrested for dealing in fake currency in a country like Argentina. I'm about to turn tail and get the hell out of there when the guy spots me and, casually flicking away his cigarette, walks over to shake my hand. He introduces himself as Fernando. 'What about the cops?' I ask.

He glances over at them as though he hadn't even noticed them. 'Oh, don't worry about them,' he says. 'But let's walk if they're making you feel uncomfortable.'

We stroll down a busy shopping street and quickly the police officers are out of sight. 'We don't worry about the cops,' Fernando explains. 'I buy most of my stock from them anyway.' He laughs. 'Well, not those guys, their bosses. Many of the deals I do are with senior officers in the Federal Police.' I wonder if he's just bragging. Or could this be true? It's hard to believe but then, at the same time, there's so much money to be made, who knows?

I'm carrying five thousand pesos because I want to show I'm serious. I hand it over to Fernando and he passes me ten thousand (fake) pesos in exchange. I'm interested in how the notes usually find their way onto the streets. Is it all taxis? 'No, not just taxis,' he says. 'I have a network of distributors to pass the notes off to. Taxis, yes. But also strip clubs, cafes, bureaux de change, anyone who can move falsos without getting caught. Someone who comes into contact with tourists is the best.' I'm struck by how young he is, late twenties, smartly dressed and good-looking. He's no gangster that's for sure.

We reach the end of the road and Fernando shakes me by the hand. I have one more question for him. These notes are made by someone. Someone who knows how to set the presses and make the paper and the ink and everything else that goes into a good counterfeit bill. I know that isn't easy or we'd all be printing off next month's mortgage on the printer at home.

He pauses for a moment. I think he's worked out that I'm not an average punter. But a smile crosses his face. 'Yes, there's a guy,' he says. 'A very important man. Very important. He makes the money.'

'And does he have a name?' I ask.

'He's known as the Artist.'

'That's it. That's the guy I've read about. But what's his real name?' I can't exactly look up the Artist in the phone book.

'I can't tell you any more.' He shakes his head and lights another cigarette. 'We call him the Artist. Let's leave it there.'

There's often two interesting points when you're interviewing criminals. The first is the point where they stop lying and begin telling the truth. This can take thirty to forty minutes. I think it takes as long as it takes for them to become comfortable that you are not a threat. The second is the point they stop telling you the truth. I think this happens at the point that they realise that what they are saying to you is becoming a threat to themselves. Fernando has clearly reached that point. Telling me more about this 'important person' is his line in the sand.

'Good luck.' Fernando shakes my hand and disappears into the crowd.

I can't wait to get back to the safety of my hotel room to see what these fake notes look like, but more, I know that this story will not be complete until I find out who is 'the Artist'.

The next morning, back at the hotel I begin to examine the handiwork of the Artist. I compare the notes I bought on the street with some of the other fake notes I've picked up while I've been in town. There's a lot of variation. At one end of the scale there are some pretty terrible copies (maybe the printer at home isn't such a bad idea after all). You can spot a bad counterfeit because the paper feels too thick, or the ink rubs off on your hand, or the watermark is off centre or even non-existent. But the better ones, like the stack of hundreds made by the Artist that I picked up last night, are a different kettle of fish altogether.

Holding up the Artist's hundred-peso bills next to a genuine hundred-peso bill, it's very very hard to tell them apart. The paper feels identical, the image and the typeface are the same, even the watermark is exactly as it should be. Whoever this man is, he's in a different league.

I put in a call to a journalist friend of mine who works for *Clarín*, one of the major papers in Buenos Aires. I ask him to look back at their articles for a mention of a counterfeiter who went by the name of the Artist. A few hours later he calls me back with a lead. In 2007, a news report described the arrest and prosecution of a gang of counterfeiters. A house was raided and the police found printing presses, plates, paper, ink and all the items necessary to produce hundreds of thousands of fake bills. The guy who owned the house, who was arrested on the spot, went by the nickname the Artist. His real name was Hector Fernandez.

I do a bit more digging into Hector Fernandez and find that 2007 wasn't his first arrest. He's been convicted five times. He has form stretching back to the early nineties, when he used to run with some pretty serious Argentine gangsters. But his rap sheet is unusual.

The longest he's served in prison is four years, despite on one occasion being caught in possession of 2 million US dollars' worth of fake notes. For a crime of that magnitude, with several previous offences, they should have locked him up and thrown away the key. But instead he's free as a bird and living in José C. Paz., a northern suburb of town. Whoever this guy is, he has friends in high places.

Two days later, my friend calls to say that he's made contact with Hector and that a meeting is on. Hector Fernandez, the Artist, forger of millions of dollars' worth of counterfeit bills is willing to meet me. At his house.

I arrive with some trepidation. Over the past twenty-four hours, I've read more about Hector. He was an associate of Daniel Bellini, an Argentine gangster known as the 'King of the Night' who is currently serving a life stretch for murdering his ballerina girlfriend. You couldn't make this stuff up. I wonder why he's agreed to meet me.

My car drops me outside a white chocolate-box-style detached house with a large mechanised gate on a street full of houses with large mechanised gates. The guy behind the wheel points out that the footballer Carlos Tevez lives round here, so you get the idea of the kind of neighbourhood we're talking about. I press the buzzer at the gate and say my name into a small intercom. The gate swings open to a long driveway that winds its way up to the front door. As I approach, standing there waiting for me, is a little old man.

Have you seen the TV show *The Sopranos*? Remember what Tony Soprano's psychopathic old uncle Junior used to look like and we have a starting frame of reference for Hector. If you haven't, then think of a little old bald man in his late sixties, smartly dressed in slacks and a pressed white shirt, sporting a pair of thick wide-rimmed spectacles.

'What a lovely house you have,' I say. I'm not kidding.

'It's not my house,' he says. 'Well, not my main house. My wife lives in my main house. She kicked me out. So now I live here.' He leads me through to the garden. There's a pool surrounded by large bougainvillaeas bursting with pink flowers. We sit along a wooden bench. 'She presented me with an ultimatum. If I wanted to carry on with my life, my profession, then I had to leave the house. I had to choose. And in that situation I preferred to leave my house.'

'You didn't love your wife?' I ask.

'I love my job.'

I explain a little to Hector about why I'm here and how I chanced across his name. As a bit of an icebreaker I show him some of the counterfeit bills I've come across already in Buenos Aires. I'm interested to know if he recognises any of them. He looks at them in turn. 'Bad,' he says of the first one. 'Bad. Bad. Very bad.' He hands each one back to me after the most cursory of inspections. 'It's really madness, madness that you can pass all of these in Argentina. Even the worst ones.'

'They're not yours then?'

'No. Not mine. I have stopped working.'

'And yet the people on the street still claim that they are made by you. You've become a myth?'

'Yes. Perhaps. It makes me feel proud. Stupidly, perhaps,' he says. Then he repeats it. 'Stupidly.'

Hector explains how things were back in the 1980s. He developed his early career as a forger with the support of various government agencies opposed to president Menem. They provided him with the presses and the paper to make fake bills, to destabilise the economy but more importantly, make them personally rich. He got caught a few times but never spent very long behind bars because he was too valuable a resource to be wasted. 'There are always arrangements that can be made.' He gives a wry smile. 'Apart from death, you can fix everything here.'

After a while Hector became more ambitious and began to forge dollars. He fell in with Bellini and began working for his gang. 'I made over ten million dollars in counterfeit for them.' He looks proud. 'Before Daniel went inside for murdering his wife. They're all nasty characters now, I'm afraid. At first you think they are good but soon you realise they are all criminals, junkies, the opposite of what you thought.'

I wonder how Hector feels about the victims of his crimes, especially tourists. I'm surprised when he says that he doesn't think about them because he never meets them. 'I never cheated a poor man,' he proudly asserts. And he never met a tourist so why should he care about them? But then his face falls. 'It is when my money is used to buy drugs that I feel guilty,' he says. 'I am anti-drugs.' He goes on that a neighbour's daughter used some of his bills a few weeks ago to buy some narcotics. But that the deal went wrong and the girl is now dead. 'A girl died because of drugs. Drugs bought with my money. Then. Then I feel guilty.'

I note that three weeks ago is pretty recent. Recent enough to sound like he's still in the business. He looks annoyed. Maybe at himself for such loose talk. Either way he becomes elusive. 'That's a temptation. But knowing what is the end, I don't want to do it any more. The end is very bad.' He trails off. He seems very frail all of a sudden.

I wonder how much he's made personally out of the millions of dollars he's made for others in his life. 'I always earned thirty per cent,' he says.

Thirty per cent of $10 million. 'So, where's your three million then?' I ask.

He laughs. 'I've spent it. Much of it on better presses. Better techniques. It haunted me if bills came out less than perfect. I spent a lot of time and money in pursuit of perfection.'

I don't know what to believe. This gentle old man sitting beside me seems a million miles away from the hardened gangster I thought I'd find at the top of the food chain. But Hector portrays himself as merely a foot soldier. Albeit a foot soldier with a gift. Hector's house is adorned with several of his paintings. Large oils and watercolours on canvases. One painting of a roaring lion hangs proudly on the wall of his living room. 'The hard part of this business is to get the bills onto the legal market,' Hector says as I admire the picture. 'That is where the real money is made. That is where there is violence and guns. I never fired a gun in my whole career.'

I'm pretty moved by Hector. I believe him when he says that he's never fired a gun. And I believe that his sadness over the dead girl is real. I imagine there have been other dead girls too. There's a sadness in Hector's eyes that maybe betrays a degree of regret at how things have played out. I see a man who is passionate and creative but has perhaps come to look back at his life and realised that there were many negative consequences to his chosen art form.

That night as I'm lying in bed wondering whether being a forger is quite so glamorous after all, I get a call from my journalist friend. He says that Hector wanted to let me know that he enjoyed our talk. He also says that he's had a call from the Buenos Aires police. I have been summoned to meet a senior officer in the serious crime squad because he 'wants a word'. Tonight.

I get out of bed and take a walk. One of the things that really strikes me about Buenos Aires is its refuse issues. On the one had, the people of BA are clearly very litter conscious; they pile their rubbish in bin bags on street corners every evening. But while the city has definitely got the hang of disposal, their collection skills haven't really caught up because the bags just seem to stay piled up for days on end. I'm mulling this over as I walk along the street to my rendezvous with the Buenos Aires crime-squad officer. I come around the corner and immediately see the biggest man I've seen since I arrived in Buenos Aires.

The guy is enormous. Biceps the size of my thighs. Chest the size of a bear's. No neck. At all. He has a baseball cap pulled down low over his eyes to such an extent that I get the distinct impression that he doesn't want to be recognised. Perhaps he should have thought of that before he bench-pressed half of Argentina.

My asking questions around town these last few days has attracted some attention. The officer wants to know why I came to BA. I don't tell him that I met with Hector Fernandez yesterday. He tells me that he knows I met with Hector Fernandez yesterday. So either he's following me or he knows the same people Hector knows. He has a message for me. 'You're starting to understand how big a problem counterfeit money is in Argentina,' he says. 'But you must also understand that this is run by large organised gangs that work at a high level.' I can feel a warning coming on. 'These people are very dangerous. They have dangerous weapons, more dangerous than the police, even.' Here comes the warning. 'These people don't joke around. If they discover you, they won't hesitate to shoot you. Then cut you into pieces and put you inside a bin bag.'

I'll never look at those bin bags the same way again.

I have a couple more days in Buenos Aires and in many ways I have already found what I came for. I have met the Artist, Hector Fernandez, the most notorious forger in South America. But something is still bugging me. The quiet man I met in his garden and the good-looking young man I met in the street don't tally with the tales of people that will cut you up and dispose of your body. They aren't the guys that Hector described as nasty people. I wonder who are those guys?

I send a message to Hector. With an intro from the Artist himself, could I maybe meet the guys from the gang who do the dirty work? The very same men who the cop warned me last night not to go looking for.

This is a big step for me. I have met many criminals and interviewed lots of bad men around the world but there is always a line that I know not to cross in pursuit of a story. That line is what I call the gang line. Gangs are ubiquitous throughout Latin America and indeed the wider world. The best known, of course, are the drug cartels in Mexico, which are notorious for murdering journalists who try to uncover their activities. But even outside of Mexico, I know things become infinitely more dangerous once you cross the gang line.

I never found out whether it was down to Hector or not but my friend calls with good news. He has received a message with very clear instructions. I am to drive to a housing project in one of the roughest districts of the city and await further instructions. Under no circumstances am I to be armed or bring any security. The men I want to meet are insisting on keeping their identities secret and they will definitely be armed. My friend recommends against going but says on the balance of probabilities he thinks I will be okay. But he offers no promises. 'Gangsters are always unpredictable,' he says helpfully.

I could tell you about how I tossed and turned all night, weighing up the pros and cons of whether or not to go to the meeting. I could tell you I was terrified about the potential consequences of meeting an armed Argentine gang at an undisclosed location. But that wouldn't be true. I never hesitated for a second. From the second I got that call, all I could think about was how tantalisingly close I was to completing the circle and finding the last piece of the puzzle. I was adrenalised for sure but I was single-mindedly focused on the prize. The decision was made in that instant. Of course I would go.

The next evening, I drive with my buddy through the rundown suburbs of BA. Tenement blocks and low-rise social housing provide shelter for the city's working classes. These are poor districts a million miles from the European-style grandeur of the centre.

Several times we receive text messages refining our destination until eventually we arrive at the agreed point and wait. It is nearly midnight and I've been sitting in the car for a few hours when the call comes. My friend is not invited. He is to deliver me to the front door of an address where I am to take the lift to the third floor and wait for someone to collect me. As we get out of the car and cross the street towards the door, I can feel myself shaking. I look down at my hand trembling and realise that in sharp contrast to last night's bravado, I am in fact now terrified.

The fear doesn't abate any when the elevator doors open and I see that a young Argentine youth is waiting for me. He looks me up and down and calls me to follow him. We walk silently together down a long hallway and eventually stop at a door where he gives three knocks. From inside I can hear first one, then two and three large deadlocks being unbolted inside. Then the door swings open and the boy gestures for to me to enter. I check in with myself. I'm still trembling but still determined to do this. I take a deep breath and enter the flat. The door shuts behind me and standing behind it is a man in what I can only describe as a latex horror zombie mask. He locks all three bolts on the door again, frisks me for weapons and pushes me firmly into the next room.

The next room is not what I was expecting.

Where to begin?

It is hot. Really hot. As well as masked man number one who I just met, there is masked men numbers two and three. ONE and TWO are carrying handguns, which they are waving around indiscriminately, shouting in heavy Argentine slang, and THREE is carrying a pump-action shotgun. I can see him eyeballing me through his latex mask from the corner of the room. There are counterfeit notes all over the room, which I wonder may have been laid out to impress me. It seems strange that they're just laid out like this.

It takes me a minute to take everything in. I try to work out what everyone is shouting about. The guys are shouting that they are in a hurry and they don't have time for this shit. 'Okay? Okay?' they keep aggressively asking me while pointing their firearms in my face. Everyone seems extremely anxious.

I'm breathing heavily while I start to explain that I only have a few questions. I say I'm happy to get started right away. I say it won't take long. This seems to placate them a little. Okay, let's get started. I'm about to fire away with my first question but they're distracted again. I'm not sure what to do. Then I realise that they aren't looking at me. They're each taking a huge noseful of cocaine from the pile of powder that I've only just noticed on the table behind them. Everything feels tense again.

With a massive sniff, ONE, who I can see now is the main guy, pumps out his chest and waves his gun at me to start with the questions.

'Is this all counterfeit?' I point to the bills piled up on the table in front of me.

'Yes, all of it,' he tells me with another loud sniff. I imagine the coke hitting the back of his throat and the buzz filling his brain.

'Can I touch it?' I lean forward to have a feel of one of the bills.

Things go into overdrive. My friend has forgotten to fully relay all of the dos and don'ts to me, and one really important rule, it turns out, is that I am, under no circumstances, to attempt in any way to touch the money. So when I reach out to touch the money, the huge guy in the corner suddenly decides to cock his pump-action shotgun as a warning for me not to break the fucking rules. It has the dual effect of making me not touch the money and also send me close the edge.

I can be guilty of getting caught up in things. I've always been like this. Once I focus on a goal, I find it hard to let go of the race to get it. But right now, I'm having to consider the very real possibility that my search for the truth about forged currency in Argentina is going to get me hurt. This situation has become way too unpredictable for comfort. It's one thing to interview an old villain at his nice house by the pool, but it is quite another to be in a locked room with coked-up guys who are waving guns around like crazy men. This situation has undoubtedly got out of hand.

My head is spinning. I start to actually consider whether I'm going to die in this room just like the cop told me I would. Am I going to be piled up on a Buenos Aires street corner with all the other bin bags waiting days for collection? Then it hits me. What is it that's so important about these guys anyway?

That's it. That's the moment the penny drops somewhere deep inside me. The moment when the purpose of my trip to Buenos Aires comes hard and fast into sharp focus. These guys are important to me. They're so important to me that I've risked my life to find out more about them. So I'd better get on with finding out what I need to know quickly and get out of here.

I just start asking questions. How do you do this? How do you get away with it? How much money do you make from it? Who supports you? Who resists you? And what happens to the people who resist you?

For a moment I hope that these are the kind of

questions that they're expecting me to ask because if not, then God knows what happens next.

I have their attention. They start to talk. Maybe it's the drugs. Maybe they just want to get something off their chests. Maybe it is all bragging, but they're talking.

The main guy says he comes from a background of kidnapping and armed robbery. 'I grew up in the streets,' he says. 'I know a lot of things. But this is how you get the biggest profits.' Now he says they control the distribution of much of the city's counterfeit currency. They use machines that are exactly the same as the ones used by the Central Bank. Someone on the inside supplies them with the paper and ink, which means that there is no difference with the originals. 'Do you like these ones?' He points to the notes in front of me. 'These ones are getting dry. See? We've got the same paper, the same ink, we've got everything.'

'And how much of this can you make in say a week? A hundred thousand pesos?' I suggest.

The room fills with laughter. I can feel it relieve some of the tension in the room. 'We make that in a day,' he says. 'We have a lot of distribution to fill. Taxis, bureaux de change, even banks.'

'Banks?' I'm shocked.

More laughter. 'Yes, even banks will buy the good ones for fifty per cent. You think just because the money comes out of the ATM that it is genuine? You're wrong.

There are many people involved in this business. People in power. We are not alone.'

'And the police? Have you ever had problems with the police?'

'Yes. Yes. Once or twice. This one.' ONE motions to TWO. 'This one was shot by the police, but he shot them back.'

TWO lifts his shirt to show me the scar across his stomach. 'He shot me here.' And then he points his finger straight to the middle of my forehead. 'And I shot him there.'

I'm lost for words.

'Clear?' he asks me.

'Yes. Clear.' I repeat.

It is time to leave.

I leave the way I came in, down the hallway, down in the lift, across the street and back to my car. I get in the car with my waiting friend and silently we drive away from one of the most terrifying experiences of my life.

In the cold sober light of day, I begin to realise how disturbed those men really were. They laughed at their own violence with a casual disdain for their victims; fuelled by cocaine they exuded bravado, and high on their own hype, they acted as though life is cheap and money is theirs to take whenever and however they want. I had no doubt that cutting me up and putting me in one of those bin liners would have been my fate if I had provoked the wrong reaction from one of them. Hector Fernandez's recommendation probably got me in the door and maybe his reputation kept me alive but still: when there's drugs and guns involved, accidents do happen.

My view of the gentleman forger that I'd held true from all those black-and-white movies now seems naive and a little stupid. The idea that there are pacifist criminals who engage in honourable victimless crimes is maybe old-fashioned now. Because for every Hector Fernandez there are three guys in latex masks wielding guns, snorting coke and shooting cops in the head.

Argentina has a problem of epidemic proportions. The control of money is rightly kept behind carefully guarded locked doors in most civilised countries in the world. There's a reason Fort Knox has its reputation. Maybe once upon a time, counterfeiting here had a noble attachment to liberal freedom fighters struggling to overthrow the cruel shackles of fascism, but that is a time long since forgotten. The criminals have taken over and now every time you get in a cab in Argentina you might only be two degrees of separation away from a masked man carrying a gun.

CHAPTER THREE

WELCOME TO MOLLYWOOD

'Hi. Are you an actor?'

'WHAT'S YOUR DREAM? Everyone who comes to Hollywood has a dream.'

This was allegedly a favourite pickup line used by hustlers to entice budding young starlets as they stepped off the buses in Los Angeles in the 1950s. They'd try to get their grubby mitts on whatever savings these wide-eyed young innocents had brought from home by promising access to producers and casting directors. If you were a kid from Nowheresville with a head full of dreams, arriving in the big city for the first time, a friendly face with a pocket full of contacts was irresistible. Unfortunately, most had to learn the hard way that dreams often just don't come true.

Of course, LA's movie industry is a much more sophisticated beast these days. You don't walk into a studio and hope to be spotted any more. But then LA doesn't have the only movie industry in the world any more either. Mumbai has a pretty good one too.

Mumbai is big. One of the word's top ten biggest cities, depending on how you count the numbers. But by any count, there's over 15 million souls blowing around. It's the 'go-to' city in India in much the same way as LA used to be in the USA. It's where you go to follow your dreams if you're a young Indian kid with ambitions to make a name or a fortune for yourself.

I'm in town to look into a modern twist on the old LA movie scam that I've read about in Mumbai guidebooks. As I walk out of the airport, I try to imagine what it was like to be one of those budding stars of the silver screen. How exciting to get discovered and bag the big role that makes you a star. A small little chap approaches me and offers to take my bag. Still lost in the fantasy, perhaps, I let him. I casually hand over my bag and carry on walking towards my adoring public. Of course, someone should carry my bag, I'm a movie star. Hello, Mumbai!

Back in reality, I realise he's a taxi driver.

Mumbai's taxis are black-and-yellow Fiats. They're rounded and small so they look a lot like toy cars. My driver fits it perfectly. I'm pretty beat from the flight and keen to get some shuteye so I give him the name of my hotel and ask him to step on it. He gives me that characteristic Indian shake of the head that everywhere else in the world means 'no' but for some reason here means, 'okay'.

Mumbai is hot. Searingly hot. The mercury is over 40°C and because the city is built along the coast and monsoon is nearly due, the humidity has risen to over

90 per cent. It's like walking around inside a kettle. My shirt is already sticking to my back by the time we reach the car.

I'm a little disappointed, to say the least, that the vehicle has no air-conditioning.

The toy taxi pulls out of the airport and I tell the toy-sized driver to hot foot it towards the highway. The drive to town should take around forty minutes and I'm already dreaming of a cold shower and some fresh linen sheets. We navigate the airport exit but before we reach the main road, a guy steps out into the road, waiving his arms around like a maniac. It's clear he's desperate for us to stop. I'm so hot that I'd happily just mow him down but the driver has other ideas. Annoyingly, he slows the car and the guy leans in the passenger window.

He's plump and a bit sweaty and he's got bulging eyes like a cartoon character that's just been bashed over the head. I'd guess he's in his early thirties and he's wearing a salmon-pink shirt and slacks. He's also carrying some kind of folder. He leans in further to take a look at me, then he gives me the most cursory of glances and goes back to his chat with the driver. It's all in Hindi so I've no idea what it is they're discussing but I wish they'd hurry up and get it over with so we can get going.

Suddenly he jumps into the passenger seat and before I can say anything, we take off again.

'Excuse me. Who are you? And what are you doing in my taxi?' Both reasonable requests I feel, given the circumstances.

'I am your travel agent,' says my new companion. He leans over from the front seat, hands me a clutch of paperwork from his folder and continues to talk matter of factly, as though there is nothing at all unusual about him being in my cab. 'Please fill in these papers.'

He explains the forms have to be completed by every tourist on arrival in Mumbai but a cursory glance is all I need to see that they are not official. They have no letterhead, they're written in terrible English and the spelling is littered with errors. I'd bet my house on the fact that he's printed them off himself. But he looks me dead in the eye, places his hand across his heart and repeats in the most solemn of voices that he is my official travel agent, already assigned to my 'case' and I have no option but to engage his services and fill in the forms.

I look again at the scraps of paper in my lap and notice that one of them mentions a twenty-dollar fee. I think I've just realised what's going on.

'That's the RTO fee, sir. Road Traffic Cooperation. Because it is your first time in India you must pay this to the road traffic officer.'

It isn't my first time in India but this could be a long journey so let's play along.

'Sir, I am a respected travel agent. When Brad Pitt and Angelina Jolie came to India, I was their travel agent too.'

I wonder if they had to pay twenty dollars.

'Yes, sir, of course.'

He's playing it deadpan. No hint of a smile crosses his face. I've come across some chutzpah before but this guy takes the biscuit. Despite everything he says sounding preposterous, he's giving it 100 per cent commitment.

'What was Brad Pitt like?' I ask him.

'Very good man. Very very good,' he says. 'Now if you want to go to a hotel, I have some very good hotels I will show you.'

'But I already have a hotel booked,' I tell him. 'I don't need another hotel.'

For no apparent reason, the taxi pulls off the highway and takes a smaller road into a rundown-looking neighbourhood. This doesn't look like the kind of district my hotel would be in. Why are we pulling off the highway? 'Traffic,' he says. 'The road ahead is blocked, so we're going to take another road.' Before I have time to argue, he suggests that I give him a tip!

'What would I give you a tip for?' I ask. He ignores the question.

'Please sir, fill in the form and give me the eleven thousand rupees.'

Eleven thousand rupees is around two hundred dollars so the price just went up by 900 per cent.

'Maybe I should just give the form and the money directly to the road traffic officer,' I suggest.

'Where are you going to find a road traffic officer?' He rolls his eyes at my idea.

'Well exactly, because if I'm not likely to meet him and he knows nothing about me, then why do I need to worry about him at all?'

'Because, sir, if you do not pay him then I will have to pay him myself.'

Emotional blackmail. New twist. I'm trying to keep a sense of humour but suddenly we come to a stop. It's too hot for this. We're on a dirt road in the middle of a poor district, flanked by low-rise concrete buildings on either side and not a hotel in sight. The taxi has been stopped in its tracks by a crowd of men who are dancing in the middle of the street and who begin to surround the car.

The 'travel agent' gets out. The men start banging drums and ringing bells and tambourines. When my friend gets back into the car, he has a worried look on his face.

'Sir, they are saying you cannot get through.' He shakes his head defeated.

Why not?

'It's a religious ceremony,' he says.

Okay, so we'll turn around and go another way.

'No sir, this is a one-way street.' He says. Completely seriously.

There is no way on earth that this dirt road in a

beat-up impoverished suburb of Mumbai is a one-way street. But the taxi driver is clearly under orders not to turn around. The crowd have now started banging loudly on the roof of the cab, which makes thinking difficult and it's all starting to feel pretty intimidating. The travel agent gets out again and disappears into the crowd. I sit and gaze out of the window into the faces of the dancing men.

How have I ended up in this situation? There's a crazed look about these guys and a frenetic energy to their dancing. One of them starts banging on the window. It's like I've landed in a zombie apocalypse. I'm actually pretty relieved to see the travel agent return. He might be a pain in the ass but he's less threatening than these guys. He's followed by a man dressed in white robes and matching turban.

'Sir, this is the holy man,' he says.

'Can we come through?' I ask the holy man.

'No,' says the holy man, wagging his finger at me. 'Religion.'

Napoleon said religion is what stops the poor from murdering the rich but right now it's close to the other way around.

'We must be able to do something.' I'm still trying to reason my way out of this.

The travel agent has a suggestion. 'Sir, he says if you want to go, you pay fifty-one thousand rupees (US$1,000) and then you can go.'

What? How much?

I'm about to explode when I see another car approach from the opposite direction. The crowd parts and it drives past us.

'Why can that car pass through?' I ask. 'And how come it can drive the other way down this "one-way street" and I didn't see him pay anyone a single rupee?' The holy man walks away. The travel agent follows. I am alone again.

Suddenly, the religious festival kicks into another gear. The banging and ringing gets faster and louder. Everyone begins to dance like lunatics, twirling around and banging on the car windows. The travel agent has even joined in. I'm sitting in a boiling hot taxi, it's nearly forty-five degrees outside, we have no air-con and nobody looks like they have any intention of moving. I try screaming to the taxi driver to get back in the car but he stares back at me blankly. I could try to get out and walk but I'm miles from the main road. Plus in this heat, I wouldn't last ten minutes.

I've been kidnapped and they want one thousand dollars to let me go.

I start to count the cash in my wallet to see how much I have. Then the holy man reappears and begins to chant prayers in my face while drawing a red Bindi on my forehead. He wraps a bangle around my wrist and blesses me. I've got to give him credit for his commitment to the role.

The travel agent reappears and implores me again to just pay up.

'Sir, it is very hot,' he says.

'Don't tell me it's hot!' I'm starting to get cross. 'You are kidnapping me.'

'Sir, you are not kidnapped. I am with you. And I am the travel agent,' he says with complete innocence. 'But please pay him and then we can go.'

I feel as though I am stuck in a Kafka-esque nightmare. I cannot progress without paying my kidnapper the ransom and yet he tells me that I am not being kidnapped. I am in a roasting tin of a taxi with a holy man and outside the window is a dancing travel agent. I don't feel scared for my safety and yet I am so powerless that I don't feel free either. I can see I'm just going to have to pay up. But not one thousand dollars. This is India after all. Haggling is acceptable, even if it is over your ransom fee.

I decide to start low. I open with an offer to the holy man of forty pounds. I flash the notes in front of him and he takes the wad. He counts it. He shakes his head. Was that a yes or a no? The travel agent appears, leaning in through the window on the other side of the cab. The holy man says something to the travel agent in Hindi and then walks away. The travel agent follows him and they disappear into one of the buildings.

I'm not sure what is going on. Have I made a faux pas? Have I offended him with my 6 per cent offer? They both return and the holy man addresses the crowd. Is he giving the order to lynch the white guy? Maybe not. Because all at once, he claps his hands and the crowd disperses. The men begin to pack up their drums and their bells. The religious festival is over. In seconds, the street is empty. Not a soul. The travel agent jumps back in the car, the taxi driver starts up the engine and we drive on as though it was all just a bad dream.

After a couple of minutes we hit the highway again and the travel agent turns around again to face me. I hope this is an apology.

'Sir, I am here to solve your problems.'

'I only have one problem,' I say. 'You. You are my only problem. I was fine until I met you.'

He begins to cry. Really goes for it. In no time at all, he is weeping.

'Sir, I have so many problems,' he stutters through the sobs. 'Sir, please help me.' He points pathetically to the form on my lap.

I've been in the taxi now for over two hours. I'm dripping with sweat and exhausted from the heat. I want to get out of this cab so badly that I could kill this man in cold blood. First I need that cold shower and then I want to sleep and forget about this taxi ride from hell. I came to Mumbai to investigate the Bollywood scam but I feel as though I have landed in my own private horror film.

Suddenly we pull over by the side of the highway. The travel agent points across the street. 'Sir, this is your hotel.'

Across the highway is a hotel that is not my hotel. I have already booked and paid for my hotel in central Mumbai. But this hotel is another hotel. This is a rundown dirty-looking fleabag of a hotel on the edge of a motorway. Why would he spend all this time taking me to this hellhole?

It starts to dawn on me. Of course, the travel agent must have a relationship with this hotel. He gets a back-hander for bringing tourists here. It's just another layer to the scam.

'This is not my hotel,' I tell him.

'Sir, your hotel is closed,' he says. 'Closed for repairs. But this is a better hotel.'

And then he casually mentions that the taxi fare is two hundred dollars.

Okay. Enough is enough. It's time to call it.

I've enjoyed the show but some straight-talking is long overdue. It's time to come clean and see what happens. I explain to my guide that I haven't been entirely honest with him. I'm not an innocent tourist. I have to give him credit, this scam is one of the most inventive I've encountered, but it's still a scam. He listens to me, all the while staring innocently back at me, nodding. I think he's heard me.

'Sir,' he says, in a low, calm, steady voice. 'I am the travel agent. I am not scamming you.'

Sigh.

So we spend the next half an hour dancing the dance. I remain resolute that I will neither check into this bogus hotel nor pay the ludicrous two hundred dollars he's asking for the taxi fare. He insists that he is a bona fide travel agent and nothing else is going on. Back and forth, standing in the searing Mumbai heat next to a dusty and smoggy road. Neither side willing to back down.

This is the tricky part of the process of interviewing criminals undercover. We have reached the point where even though we both know that the other knows what is really going on, the game is still live because the criminal feels backed into a corner. The only way that he knows how to play this is to keep up the deceit. I need to make him see that I won't pay the two hundred dollars for the taxi fee or go to a bogus hotel but that he can still get something out of this situation if he plays ball. At the same time, I have to reassure him that he won't get into trouble. But until he sees that, he figures his best option is to keep up the act and hope I crack. To shake that idea out of his head takes time and persistence.

I go for the full charm offensive. I tell him that I have grown tired of taxi scams as they are so common and that I thought I had seen 'em all. Until today. I effuse about how impressed I am by the scale and imagination that was on show. I applaud his chutzpah and praise his acting chops. I say that I am as honoured to have seen his performance in the flesh as if he were Laurence Olivier doing *Hamlet* at the National Theatre.

Nothing. He's not budging.

I change tack and instead offer him a carrot. Well, a carrot and a stick. I offer to pay him half of the two hundred dollars in return for an honest explanation of what he's been up to today. And I will give my word not to report him to the police. The alternative is that we call the police now and let them settle the matter. He picks the carrot.

We climb back into the car to escape the roar of the passing traffic. He asks me not to use his name and then he begins to explain to me how his scam works. Of course, he is not a travel agent. He is a full-time conman. The men we encountered on the street are organised by him and they split whatever they get fifty–fifty. He says that he also has other stooges he can use. His favourite is an old lady who gets into the car with crippling stomach pains and begs for a lift to the hospital. 'Tourists always want to help,' he says. 'Then when we get to the doctor (also bogus, also on the payroll) and she asks for more money. Sometimes we can get people to give a hundred dollars.' She sounds like a blast. I wonder why wasn't she involved today? Ironically, he says she couldn't come today because she was sick.

He says the ultimate prize is the two-hundred-dollar taxi fare. The real fare should be five dollars. And then the cherry on top is if, he says, people check into the hotel. 'People are too tired,' he says. 'After a long flight and three hours in the hot taxi, they just want to rest. So they stay here even though they have booked another hotel. They just give up.' All in all a good day, with the commission from the hotel included, can net him over five hundred dollars.

I tell him that I'm impressed with how much performance goes into his schtick. He looks flattered. He says he got into this game many years ago and he's refined the scam over time.

'And this is Bollywood,' he says. 'Everyone in Mumbai wants to be an actor.'

'You look as though you enjoy the acting.'

'Yes, I like this work,' he smiles.

I give him the hundred dollars we agreed on.

'And I like making money,' he says.

I leave the travel agent by the side of the road and the taxi driver turns us around and back to my real hotel. I've had the rudest awakening to the potential that Mumbai has to offer. I'm tired to the point of exhaustion and I haven't even reached my hotel yet. This is going to be an exciting place to look for scams. Tomorrow I want to get back to the main reason I'm here, the Bollywood movie scam. But first I need to sleep.

*

The next morning, fresh and rested, I take breakfast on the balcony outside my room and look out across the sprawl of the city. Mumbai is a city that has an old-fashioned sense of romance about it. It's where dreamers and starlets and gangsters walk among the stray dogs. It's where beggars rub shoulders with artists and servants and fishermen. And it has more billionaires and slums than just about any other city in the world. It is also India's financial powerhouse, fashion epicentre and crucially the hub for the country's blossoming film and television industry, which we all know as Bollywood.

If Mumbai is your introduction to India, steel yourself because, while there is very little physically threatening about the place, the sheer energy of it could knock you off your feet. The heart of the city contains some exceptionally grand colonial architecture; the train station is an extravagant Gothic building with dog-faced gargoyles, turrets and spires. Around the corner are some of the most exciting and avant-garde new buildings you'll see anywhere in the world including the world's most expensive private house, with a price tag of $1 billion. Explore a little deeper and you'll uncover bazaars and temples as well as a nightlife that's buzzing with vibrant restaurants and bars.

I'm standing on the street corner near to the Colaba Causeway. It's one of the tourist-rich parts of town where there's plenty of Western faces. This is one of the spots where my guidebook warns tourists to be on their guard. I spend a couple of hours doing my best, unassuming tourist routine: standing on the corner with the guidebook and map in hand. This is the kind of legwork they don't tell you about in the job description. It's mentally tiring to look vulnerable for long periods of time. All that innocent-faced duplicity really takes it out of you.

People bustle past, going about their business as they would in any busy international city, but the only people I'm approached by are a couple of dead-eyed beggars, who I'm tempted to talk to just for some company. I move around the corner and see a guy looking over. He catches my eye and then comes over to say hello. He's a bit scruffy-looking and there's something about the glazed look in his eyes that makes me wonder if he hasn't been on the wacky backy. But he's the first Indian to talk to me all morning so I'm happy for the company. We deal with the usual 'are you married' issue that people in India feel obliged to ask before any other conversation can occur. Then we talk about what I am going to do while I'm in Mumbai and all the while I'm trying to work out what this guy is after. Then he casually asks me if I'm a movie star. Weird question. But I wonder if this is the start of the scam I've read about. I tell him that I am not a movie star but it's nice of him to ask. He looks a little disappointed and confidently tells me that I look like one, which seems like a genuine compliment. But I've barely time to say thank you before he says his goodbyes and leaves. And I find myself feeling disappointed. Firstly that he didn't try to scam me. And secondly that I was inherently suspicious of the nice guy on the street who was only being friendly.

I decide to take a break and grab some lunch nearby. Afterwards I'm still thinking about that last interaction when a pretty, smartly dressed young woman comes over to me and says, 'Hi. Are you an actor?' Now, that is a coincidence and I don't believe in coincidences. Either I got out of the right side of bed this morning, or there's something going on. My radar kicks in and I start to wonder if the guy I met earlier wasn't some kind of spotter. I do hope so. I revert to innocent tourist mode and with my best false modesty face, I tell the nice lady that I am not an actor, but I try to look charmed by the suggestion.

'You can be,' she says. Not 'you could be' or 'you should be' but 'you can be', which strikes me as a strange way to put it. 'I'm not kidding. Guys who look like you are in demand at the moment.'

White guys? Isn't Bollywood more of an Indian thing?

'Doesn't matter,' she says. 'Don't you know Katrina Kaif or Amy Jackson? They aren't Indian and they are the biggest stars in Bollywood right now.'

My new fan introduces herself. Her name is Molly. She's a casting director. And, she explains, her job is to find new talent. If I have time, she'll buy me a coffee and tell me how I can become a star. I strongly suspect this is the start of a scam. But Molly isn't like any scam artist I've ever met before. She's confident, charming and slick and she's a woman. I imagine she has a pretty good hit rate. Who wouldn't enjoy being stopped on the street by a charming casting director who wants to tell them they could be the next Katrina Kaif? I have no idea who Katrina Kaif is. But I bet she's rich.

Either I'm wrong and she's about to make me a star or I'm right and this is a scam. I'm game to find out which, so I agree to go with Molly to a cafe called Leopold's, where she says we can talk. Over iced coffee, Molly tells me that she is casting a new movie, which is shooting imminently. She is passionate and earnest. She says that the movie is going to be really great. Right now, they're almost ready to go but she's still short one foreigner. She says that it has become *de rigueur* for Indian films to feature a foreign actor as it gives the production a certain cachet. Exotic even. The guy who was supposed to play the part has dropped out last minute, which is why she's been hanging out looking for a good-looking Westerner with star quality. Those are her words, not mine, but I'm not arguing. Molly says in this part of town the cafes are famously filled with actors waiting to be spotted, sort of unofficial casting lounges. In fact, she says she was surprised that I wasn't deliberately hanging around there waiting to get picked up by someone just like her.

Molly could be an LA scam artist right out of the 1950s. And as far as she's concerned, right now I'm a wide-eyed starlet gagging for fame and fortune. At least, that's what I'm hoping she thinks. Really, I'm intrigued to find out how she's going to spin this to make money.

Molly says that she's sure the director of the movie will 100 per cent go for me but we still have to approach it professionally. Her first question is whether or not I have a portfolio of pictures. She says this is essential to show to the director. Obviously that's not something the average Joe takes away on holiday but, no problem, I have an idea. I suggest that I can take some shots on my iPhone and print them off at a Snappy Snaps. She shakes her head. 'That won't work at all. It's professionals we are talking about.'

What can I do? I'm in a town where I know nobody and I don't have a camera other than the one on my phone.

But would you believe it? Molly has just the solution. 'We can do something.' She starts scanning through the numbers on her phone. She finds one. 'We can quickly go and shoot a portfolio for you today. But we'll need to find a photographer and none of them will do it for free. So are you willing to shell out some money?'

Ah ha. Here we are. The bit where I start paying over the money. This is more like it.

'Sure,' I say, trying to look as excited as I possibly can. 'Why not?'

She smiles. She seems convinced that I'm into it and she dials the photographer. Moments later the 'casting director' is negotiating my portfolio with the 'photographer' so we can send my headshot to the 'director'. If only she knew that the real performance was happening right in front of her. I give her my best overexcited double thumbs-up face.

Molly gets off the phone and she's smiling. The guys are going to do me a deal. As long as we can use my hotel as a location, then he'll shoot and deliver a full portfolio for four hundred pounds. Molly reassures me that that's a bargain. It sounds expensive to me. But she reminds me that I'll make that back in a little over a day. Gotta invest in myself if I want this. I ask if I have time to mull it over but she says no. My shoot is going to start tomorrow so I need to fix this today.

'You have to make up your mind very quickly,' she says.

Her job is to deliver someone by close of play today so it's now or never. Up to me. Moment of truth. I pretend to play it over in my mind for the right amount of time. Of course I'm going to do this. If I'm right, then it's exactly the scam that I came to Mumbai to uncover. I pretend I'm being brave and tell her that I've decided to 'go for it'. She gives me a high five. We'll meet in my hotel lobby with the photographer in an hour.

Back at the hotel, I meet the photographer, Aditya. 'Call me Bob,' he says as we head down to the pool. I'd love to ask Bob if he's in on the scam or whether he's a genuine photographer who's just been booked on a job. I'd love to know if this is a conspiracy that they're both in on but of course I can't risk blowing my cover to find out.

I've chosen a collection of outfits: a smart one, a casual one and a colourful one. I figure that while I play the part of tourist I might as well get my money's worth. Bob has some funky ideas about where to shoot. It all seems very legit. For a second, I find myself actually enjoying the fantasy of it. What if I really was about to do a poolside photo shoot in Mumbai for a part in a movie? That would be incredibly cool. I can almost understand how someone could be seduced into feeling like this was all for real.

Bob instructs me to 'strut my stuff'. I do a couple of what I think are catwalk poses up and down the side of the pool while he shoots off hundreds of shots. 'Good. Good,' he keeps saying encouragingly.

'You're a natural,' Molly chips in.

I've got to admit, I'm enjoying the attention and I'm actually having fun. After we've done the walking shots, Molly asks me to slip into my swimwear and we begin taking topless shots in the pool. Molly calls these 'bad boy' shots. She asks me to pout and frown and generally act like I'm James Bond. It feels ridiculous but she keeps chirping, 'Great, great.' Bob seems happy too. Everyone seems happy until Molly suddenly remembers something and the drama increases another notch.

'You don't have an actor's Equity card, do you?' she asks.

She seems genuinely concerned. She should win an Oscar. Of course I don't. On account of my not being an actor. Is it going to be a problem?

'Yes, it's a massive problem,' she says. I can feel another layer to the scam being trowelled on. 'You cannot work on set without it.'

'Is there anything we can do about it?'

'Yes.'

Phew. Thank God for that. I thought I was about to lose my big chance!

Again Molly has the solution, although it will involve (you've guessed it) a fee. 'We will have to get your card made quickly,' she says. How much? 'Around three hundred pounds but we need it. And we need it quickly. Otherwise you can't shoot tomorrow.'

This is starting to add up. All in, that's seven hundred pounds. At that price, even the most foolish person might need some reassurance. 'You are definitely in the movie,' she says. 'You don't have to worry about that but we do have to pay for the union thing. There's no way around it.'

The aim of all this charade, I'm sure, is to make the mark feel pumped up. If Molly's plan has worked then by now I would already feel like a star, intoxicated by the promise of fame. If I was in that state, then sure, seven hundred pounds would not seem like a lot of cash. Just two days' wages, an investment more than a cost. Who wouldn't then want to push forward? It does all make sense. It's a no brainer.

I hand over seven hundred pounds to Molly to cover the cost of the photos and the card but she still seems stressed. She says there's no time to waste and she needs to get over to the actors union offices ASAP to fill in the paperwork on me to get my card in time. 'I have to quickly rush back, I have to show these pictures and I have to get your card made,' she says. 'That's my job and it's really getting late.'

She'll meet me in Leopold's tomorrow at 10 a.m. And we'll go together from there to the set and I can meet the director. 'Get a good night's sleep.' She kisses me goodbye on both cheeks. 'You're going to need it, superstar.'

I'm buzzing. The day has gone well. I've made real inroads into the Bollywood scam. The pickup and the photo shoot, I'm sure, are just the start. I'm now a fish on Molly's hook and I can hardly wait to see what happens next. That night, as I'm falling asleep, I'm already strategising about when best to try to flip Molly and reveal that I'm on to her. I'm wondering whether

I might even persuade her to let me have a go myself, be her accomplice for a day, maybe even play the role of photographer. I'm running through the day's events, happy I gave her every reason to suspect that I was ripe for more pickings. Tomorrow is going to be fun.

It's 10 a.m. at Leopold's the next day and I'm waiting for Molly to arrive. I'm still trying to work out where she goes next with the scam. My guess is that it will involve the director. I'm a willing and pliable mark, ready to be divested of plenty more cash in my pursuit of fame. I order myself a coffee and wait.

By 11 a.m., I realise that Molly isn't coming. I try her mobile a couple of times but each time it rings out. I ask the waiters in Leopold's if they remember her on the offchance that maybe she might be a regular customer. I consider the possibility that she thought we were to meet at 11 a.m., so I hang on for another twenty minutes. But still there is no sign of her. I must admit that I feel more than a little disappointed that she hasn't tried to capitalise on my gullibility. But as the disappointment wears off I just feel stupid that I didn't see this coming. I should have challenged her yesterday when I had the chance. Now I've lost my best lead into the Bollywood actor scam. I go back to my hotel feeling more disappointment, but this time with myself.

*

The next day I remember something Molly said. She mentioned that anyone who was anyone or wanted to be anyone hung around in the cafes in Kolrabai. If I have any chance of tracking her down, then it's probably going to be around there. It's a long shot but then what other options do I have in a city of 15 million people?

I dress up in my best, 'I wanna be a star' outfit: jeans and a shirt and a smart pair of Ray-Bans. I pick a cafe along the main strip underneath the billboards of X and Y Bollywood stars advertising Z new Bollywood release. I am not alone. On the other side of the cafe are a group of beautiful young people. All in their twenties, all trendy haircuts, shades and pouts. If you can't beat 'em, join 'em, eh?

I've got a good seat, right out next to the road, so I give every passer-by who looks vaguely movie-business-like my best pouty pose face. But all I get are a few disturbed glances. After three hours of posing, my lips are hurting and I'm beginning to feel a bit like a plonker. I guess this is the reality of trying to get spotted. I approach the group of youngsters and ask them if they're actors. They all laugh at the suggestion. No, they tell me, they're students. The actors don't get out of bed this early! If I want to spot actors in here then I need to come back later in the afternoon so I decide to call it a day.

Back in 'my spot' the next evening, the cafe is much busier and as the students said, there is more of a buzz around the place. I've brought some entertainment in case it's another long wait: a beer and a copy of the Lonely Planet guide to Mumbai. There's an interesting chapter that describes, almost to the letter, the experience I had with Molly. Once upon a time a tourist or two did genuinely get spotted and launched into a Bollywood movie simply by standing in the right place at the right time. Early Bollywood producers looking for the exotic Westerner to put in their film reckoned a tourist would do just as well as a Western actor and would cost a fraction of the price. So a modern myth developed and tourists started to believe that the same might happen to them.

Bollywood has come a long way since then and while this casual approach to casting is now a thing of the past, the myth lives on. But where there's an unmet expectation there's an opportunity and the scammers have stepped in to exploit it. Molly clearly wasn't a casting director but she knew enough of the lingo to appear like one and my seven hundred pounds was a good day's work for her. From what the guidebook says, she's not alone, and by sitting here reading it outside this cafe, I am demonstrating what these bogus casting directors are really looking for. Not talent, but vulnerability.

'Hello, do you mind if I sit here?'

I didn't even notice anyone come in. He's a slick, trendy, young Indian chap with a leather jacket and some groovy-looking shades. He's ordering a Coke and checking the mails on his BlackBerry. I'm not sure he's even looked at me. I carry on reading my book. 'Excuse me, are you an actor?' he interrupts. Oh hello.

There's something I love about these moments. When you have set yourself as bait and you get a bite on the line. It surprises me every time.

'No, I'm not an actor,' I tell him. 'Why do you ask?'

'You look like an actor,' he says. 'And I know. Because I'm a casting director.'

Tony tells me that he has a movie that he's working on, the director is a top up-and-coming guy, the movie is shooting this week, there is a part for a foreigner but the actor they had has dropped out at the last minute. Tony thinks I have exactly the look they need. This is almost verbatim the same spiel that Molly used, but Tony's version has one twist. He doesn't need photos from me. No. He would need me to do a short screen test! My first thought is how much is that going to cost me. But he spikes my curiosity when he tells me it won't cost me a penny. He'll cover it. Hmm. This is an interesting variation.

We jump into Tony's car and drive just a few blocks down the road to a studio where he says he knows the manager. I'll have to memorise a few lines of script and deliver a performance in front of camera, which he will send to the director. If the director likes me then I'll get the part. If the director doesn't like me then nothing lost. No cost to me. If I didn't know better I'd think it was a genuine casting. I'm dying to know where the catch is.

The studio looks totally legit. It's a green screen backdrop in a small room with a camera on a tripod at one end. Tony shows me the set-up and blocks out the movements that I'll need to do as I deliver the lines. We read through the script together. I will be auditioning for the part of a British soldier who has been caught behind enemy lines by some Indian soldiers. My character knows a little Hindi so I will be expected to deliver the first line in Hindi and then three more lines in English. I've never spoken a word of Hindi before so Tony has to help me get my tongue around some of the words. When I think I have the hang of it, we can go for a take.

I did a bit of drama when I was at school. I really enjoyed it. So this is at once exciting and rather ridiculous but I decide to commit to the performance. I try to get into the mindset that even though I am 99 per cent sure that this is another scam, there is a 1 per cent chance (okay I know it's ridiculous, but let a boy dream for a minute) that this is a genuine audition and I am going to get a part in a Bollywood movie off the back of it. And in any case, there's only one way to find out, so I put my heart and soul into my audition. Tony says my Hindi is a little off and so he makes me do a few takes until I get it right. He's so insistent, that that 1 per cent starts to slowly creep up to 1.5 or maybe 2 per cent. I can't work out why he would bother to keep reshooting if it was a scam. Wouldn't he just tell me it was brilliant and move on to the bit where I hand over the money? I still haven't worked out how that's going to happen yet either. The whole thing is starting to become confusing.

It doesn't get any less confusing. When we're done and Tony is happy with a take, we leave and he drops me back to the cafe. He seems really genuinely excited about my potential and says he can't wait to get the tape across to the director. He doesn't ask me for any money. He doesn't even mention money. He just takes my number and says he'll call as soon as he has some news. We hug. He tells me I'm going to be a star. And then he leaves. So where was the scam?

I hear nothing from Tony for a couple of days. And then I get a call. It's THE CALL! The director saw my tape. Yes. The director loves what I did. NO WAY. The director wants to cast me in his movie. IS THIS A JOKE? No. No joke. Tony insists this is a genuine offer. We're good to go. We're going to make a movie. We should celebrate. I tell him to come over to my hotel this evening. I'll put some champagne on ice. I put the phone down and feel a palpable sense of relief. Phew. Here comes the scam. I'm back on familiar territory.

Tony turns up on time that evening with a young Asian woman in a party frock. I'd say she's in her early twenties and she says she's an actress too. Her name is Melody.

She seems really sweet but because I can't work out how I am about to get scammed, I am still a little on edge. Tony still seems pretty pumped, he can't stop telling me what an amazing opportunity this is for me so we crack open the champagne, make a toast to the movie business and I feel myself begin to relax. Everyone is getting along great. Melody tells me her story. She grew up in the Philippines – Indian mother, Filipino dad – and came to Mumbai to follow her dream of being an actress. So far she's had a couple of small parts in movies, which she says is all down to Tony. Tony is obviously proud of her, so proud that he gets her to stand up and do a turn, a slightly cringe-making few minutes while she does a dance audition piece. Let's just say that it's not really my bag.

But it's fun. Tony is good company and even Melody seems pleased for me, although she admits that she's a little bit jealous. I'm starting to enjoy myself as the champagne keeps flowing. I call down to room service for more and we put on some music. When the knock at the door comes, I jump up to let them in.

It isn't room service.

I've barely opened the door when two huge guys push their way in. The first guy is six four with the searing green eyes that some Indian guys have. He reminds me of Richard Kiel, the guy who played Jaws in the Bond movies. His accomplice is a heavyset bald guy carrying a clipboard. Who the hell are these guys? And what are they doing pushing their way into my room? Every minute in Mumbai seems to offer another twist in its plot.

The bigger guy points to Melody. 'Who's she?'

'Who are you?' I counter. He flashes me a badge. Police.

'Just sit down.' He points me back to my seat. 'Who else is here?' And sends the bald guy to do a quick tour of my suite.

'What are you doing here?'

So what if he's a cop? I'm still outraged at the intrusion. Tony puts a hand on my shoulder to encourage me to sit. He says quietly under his breath, 'He's a fucking cop. Just sit down. You're in Mumbai now.'

I take a breath. Be calm and sit down. I've done nothing wrong so I've no reason to cause trouble.

The big cop sits down too. He scribbles down a couple of notes and looks up to me. 'You're doing something wrong. You know? You know what?'

No I don't. I'm having a drink in my room with a couple of friends. We're not breaking any law. We're not causing anyone any trouble. What could we possibly be doing wrong?

'You have a drinking licence?' he asks in the most intimidating way possible.

'I'm over twenty-one.' I think that's pretty clear.

The cop shakes his head. 'Possession of alcohol is illegal in Mumbai without an alcohol permit,' he says. 'And the legal age for alcohol consumption here is twenty-five. There is a jail sentence of up to five years for supplying alcohol to underage people.'

I've never heard of this until now. I look to Tony. He nods to me. 'It's true,' he says.

The cop is looking closely at Melody. 'How old is she?'

Melody looks at the floor. She is silent. She looks petrified.

He points at her again. 'She's underage.'

I can't believe what I'm hearing. I've never heard of this alcohol licence before and I had no idea either that the drinking age in Mumbai was twenty-five or that Melody was under it. What the hell was Tony doing bringing an underage girl to my room?

Tony goes over to the cop and says something quietly in his ear. The cop explodes. He pushes Tony across the room and follows after him shouting angrily. I'm sure there's going to be a fight so I jump in to calm everything down. 'Come on, guys,' I say. 'Surely we can work this out. It's all a very innocent mistake.'

The cop takes Tony by the arm and says something to him in Hindi that I can't catch.

I ask Tony. 'What was that?'

Tony takes me quietly to one side. 'He says he wants two thousand dollars.' He looks really scared. 'This is serious, Conor. You need to pay this guy and get us out of here.' Then he really floors me. 'He thinks Melody is a prostitute.'

What? Suddenly a wave of calm floods over me. Of course. This is it. This is the scam. How could I not have seen it earlier? These two, maybe even three, are working together and I am the patsy in the scene. I am not going to get arrested. Melody is not underage. This is all an act for my benefit. I have to give them credit, they sucked me in for a moment. But I cannot let them see just yet that I'm on to them. I need to play along to see where it goes.

I decide to look a lot more worried. Now we're all acting out our scenes. Only we're in different movies. I turn to Tony and act terrified. Is Melody a prostitute? I ask. Tony, what the hell is going on?

'Of course she's not, man, but you don't want to be taken down to the police station with an underage girl who they think is a prostitute. Believe me. In Mumbai people don't always want to hear the truth. Better just to pay.'

I jump to my feet. I almost scream at Tony. 'This is crazy! How on earth did you get us into this situation?'

The two cops begin to talk quietly and then Melody starts to cry. I actually wonder for a minute if maybe she's an innocent caught up in the middle of all this. Then one of the cops comes over and takes her by the elbow. She looks frightened. I can't tell who's acting and who's not any more. But he leads Melody out of the door and Tony gets up to follow. 'Where are you going?' I ask. 'You can't leave me here.'

'I can't just leave her, man.' He collects his stuff and then under his breath he says, 'Just pay him some money and make it go away.'

Tony has played his part perfectly. Now he makes to exit stage left with Melody. I'm to be left alone to face the music. Alone with this huge brute sitting opposite me. I start to rerun the events of the last few days in my head: the audition, the call from Tony, his suggestion that we party together tonight, and then this guy turns up and I'm facing a two-thousand-dollar bill. A flash of doubt crosses my mind. Am I 100 per cent sure that this is the scam? My gut says that it just all seems too coincidental. Nobody has given me any clue that it's anything other than genuine but I'm beginning to learn not to trust anyone in this city. Everyone I've met here so far has a touch of the actor about them.

The 'cop' lights a cigarette and looks me dead in the eye. I have to make the call. I try to imagine what I would do if I were a tourist and I thought he was a genuine cop. I would, of course, pay him rather than have to explain this situation down at the police station. Why an underage prostitute came to be drinking in my room when the cops burst in is not exactly the kind of story you ever want to have to explain away. But as I look at him now, I see something. I have to trust my instincts. This is a scam. I am sure of it. A very elaborate scam but a scam none the less.

Suddenly I feel an urge to know all about it. It's decision time. Time to put my money where my mouth is.

I call it. I call to Tony as he's walking out the door. 'What's going on here, Tony?' He turns. 'When are we going to drop the act and admit what's really going on here?'

The cop jumps out of his seat and lurches towards me. Tony blocks him and motions to him to wait a second.

Tony runs back over to me. 'What the fuck is wrong with you?' he spits at me. Tony isn't letting his guard down.

'Sit down!' shouts the cop.

I sit down and lay out my cards. 'I'm in Mumbai on the hunt for scams,' I explain. 'And I think this whole thing is a little scene put on for me. To try to get money out of me.'

Everybody freezes. Then Tony reaches for his phone and ducks out to make a call. The cop continues to eyeball me. We sit staring at each other for a minute until Tony returns and they argue. Tony seems uncomfortable and the cop is angry with him. I can't read what is going on and then, without even a goodbye, Tony leaves. The cop and I are alone at last.

'What are you doing?' he asks me.

He glares at me for the whole time it takes me to tell him what I want. A couple of minutes without blinking. It's incredibly intense. I'm not a threat to him and I only want to ask him a few questions because I know he's not, and probably never has been, a police officer.

He nods, slowly like he's making up his mind. A dark crooked smile slides across his face and he lets out a deep booming laugh. He points a finger at me. 'Very good.' He laughs again. I think that means the scene is over and we can come out of character.

With that unpleasantness out of the way I breathe a huge sigh of relief. My fear was that he would just walk away. But I can see instead that he seems happy, eager even to talk to me.

I tell him how brilliant I thought his performance was. He gives a modest bow of the head. I tell him how he totally had me going. He seems pleased with that. And I wonder how he got into this business. Was he an actor maybe?

Ranjit lights a cigarette and begins to tell me a story about when he was a kid and got arrested by a cop. 'I hadn't done anything wrong,' he says. 'But anyway my parents had to go down to the police station and pay the cop some money to get me released. Now I think back, that's where I got the idea that you could be a fake cop and get money out of people.

'I did my first scam on my own friends,' he says. Back in 1985, Ranjit and a friend faked a stabbing on a night out. 'I used a fake knife and my partner fell to the ground.' All of his friends ran away. Then another accomplice posing as a police officer came asking questions. Ranjit convinced all his friends to put in four hundred dollars each to pay him off. 'Then we split the money.' He laughs.

I'm surprised that he would rip off his own friends.

'Of course,' he says. 'Your friends are the easiest people to fool because you know them the best.'

This is a level of cunning manipulativeness that I have not encountered before. I'd always seen sharks as predators but assumed that they chose random strangers on whom to prey. But here is Ranjit telling me about how he sees even his closest friends as viable targets. It's a new low for me to meet someone who's empathy doesn't even extend to his mates.

'Tourists too can be made fools of very easily,' Ranjit says. 'Tony and I have been working together for a couple of years now and I work with other guys like him too. Either way we can normally find one or two tourists to hit every month.' He says it's not always the Bollywood scam they use. Sometimes they'll use drugs. 'One of us will offer a tourist drugs and then the other one will turn up pretending to be the police.' Whichever method they use, the results are always the same. Most tourists would rather pay the bribe than explain themselves down at the police station where they fear they risk spending time in the cells. He says a thousand dollars is not impossible. 'It depends how scared they are.'

I wonder what would the real police say if I told them what had happened here tonight.

'It depends,' says Ranjit. 'But usually, if they find out what is going on, they would want some of the money.'

So the fake policeman would have to pay off the real policeman?

'That's it. Everyone wants to be paid. And then it is settled.'

In many ways, he seems very much like an actor to me. A man who is operating outside of himself. Maybe the role offers him a cloak of protection from his own conscience.

'Every man is an actor,' he says. 'The way you choose to use that talent is what determines how much cash you can make whether you are a salesman or a fake cop like me.' Then he fixes me with a steely look. 'With me,' he says sternly, 'when I start ...' he clicks his fingers loudly, '... I complete.'

And that I suppose is this particular actor's catchphrase.

'When I do my job,' he says, 'I execute it with confidence. And the most important thing is that I enjoy it.'

I wonder if he thinks he could play a part in Bollywood.

'Why not? If someone offers me a part. I can do anything.'

And does he think he'd be better at playing a good guy or bad? 'I could be a bad guy. But I can do comedy also,' he says in the most terrifyingly cold voice you can imagine.

What do people in his life think he does?

'They think I sell potatoes and onions.' He roars with that massive laugh again. Maybe he really could do comedy.

It strikes me that Ranjit is a master of improvisation. Sure, he's a big guy with a face like thunder and he uses those attributes to his advantage. But he says that he avoids physical confrontation at all times. His method is about intimidation and he would rather use his wits than his fists. He says he always makes a careful plan but that he and his accomplices must be ready to act around any changes in the circumstances with confidence and commitment. In the end, the goal is to convince his victim that they are in the wrong and that he is the one who can help. For a price, of course.

Ranjit is a man who knows what he wants and he's prepared to operate outside of what the rest of us would consider morally acceptable to get it. He has a loose relationship with the truth. He's a man who would rip off his friends and think nothing of it. Maybe in another life Ranjit could have been an actor on the silver screen but he chose instead to use those talents along a different path.

As I say goodbye to him and see him disappear into the Mumbai night, I reflect on my time in Mumbai. I'm pretty thrilled with all that I've uncovered here. I'm impressed even by the flair of the deceit that I've uncovered. The con artists of Mumbai are the most imaginative

I've encountered anywhere in the world. Maybe they are touched in some way by the magic of the movie industry happening all around them. Maybe the scams of a city reflect in some way the city's psyche. Either way, I feel as though I have been part of a beautifully created piece of theatre as the city has passed me from one scam-filled scene to the next.

Interactive theatre in London, where I live, has become very *de rigueur* at the moment. The idea is that it is immersive so that you get to experience performance by being a part of it. Theatre groups such as You Me Bum Bum Train and Punchdrunk spend months and months elaborately planning the details of these productions down to a tee. I think they'd be impressed by some of the scams that I've encountered here in Mumbai.

The fake travel agent and his committed performance, the casting director complete with photographer and, of course, the icing on the cake, the Bollywood casting room with celebratory wrap party, underage prostitute and fake cop. I'm certain now that all these people were merely playing roles in a series of elaborate hoaxes designed to part me from my money. And I'd have to say, they were worth every penny.

Bravo, Mumbai. Bravo.

CHAPTER FOUR

OH DANNY BOY

'This is my job because I have no fear'

I SOMETIMES WONDER, if I had to pack up my life in a hurry and hide out somewhere, what city would I choose? Barcelona often comes out on top. I'm not saying it's likely to happen, but if it did, Barcelona is definitely my kind of town. It's a passionate city: culturally exciting, great food and weather, beautiful parks, a great beach and some of the world's most striking architecture.

Barcelona's layout is what we would now call a classic grid, although it was designed in the mid-1800s by Barcelona's second most celebrated architect, Ildefons Cerdà. A feature of Cerdà's unique design was to round off the edges of buildings. It gives the place a 'look'. But really it was done for practical reasons: it afforded pedestrians better visibility when crossing the street and gave the trams, with their large turning radius, the space they needed to make it around the corners.

My favourite part of the city is Eixample, where you'll find Barcelona's most celebrated building, the Sagrada Família, built by its most celebrated architect, Antoni

Gaudí. But Gaudí never got to actually finish it, because on 8 June 1926 he walked around the corner to cross the street and in a delicious twist of architectural irony, he was knocked down by a tram. I guess Cerdà had the last laugh.

I'm not alone in liking Barcelona, because it's also the number one tourist destination in all of Spain and the third most visited city in the world after London and Paris – over 8 million visitors annually. Most of these visitors are rich Westerners like me, who come to gawp at the wonder of the Sagrada Família and soak up some sun and culture. All packed in together, 8 million tourists must appear like a shoal of sardines to the predatory shark. And in Barcelona, there is one particularly dominant type: the thief.

The few times in my life when I've had something stolen from me, it's driven me crazy. Batshit crazy. I've felt a combination of anger and hatred towards the thief but also more than a touch of self-loathing too. I blame myself for being careless. Somehow, I make it my fault that I didn't spot it happening and it can take days for me to forgive myself. I literally victim-blame myself.

But you can pick any number of books and films about train robbers, bank robbers, even bicycle thieves, and what you see is the thief portrayed as sympathetic anti-hero. There's a disconnect here. Why do we romanticise them? Especially when the thief's victim is so passive in the crime. The thief strikes while we are minding our own business. There's no element of us 'asking for it' or 'well, if you hadn't been doing that then you wouldn't have ended up in that situation' about it.

That's why I'm in Barcelona. To catch a thief and shake him until I get to the bottom of this. I've decided on here because it's the place I'm reliably informed is the best in the world to find a thief. Spain is literally full to bursting with thieves. And Barcelona is the thievery capital of Spain.

The reasons are twofold. First all those tourists make for perfect victims. Second, there is scarce legal deterrent for petty crimes in Spain. The law defines petty theft here as less than four hundred euros, for which punishments are limited to a small fine or a maximum of three days in a detention centre. No jail time unless the robbery involves violence or more than four hundred euros. And what's more, a thief's previous convictions cannot be taken into account.

Soft on crime, soft on the causes of crime. But it means there is nowhere safer for a thief to practise his art than here.

I'm already starting to wonder how I'm ever going to spot a crime that I can't see. Right now, someone in Barcelona is losing their wallet or phone or passport. In a few minutes, they'll realise that they have been robbed and those feelings of anger and self-loathing will rise up in them. There will be tears. A vacation will have been ruined in that instant. Then the practicalities will kick in: were they insured? Do they need to report it to the police? Where is the police station? An afternoon that could have been spent enjoying tapas and Rioja with friends will instead be spent filling out forms, cancelling bankcards and contacting the embassy. That drama with all its inherent tragedy is happening right now and the viewer in me desperately wishes that I was watching from a grandstand seat.

At the end of the Ramblas, one of the most popular spots in Barcelona, is the Columbus Monument. Chris Columbus on top of a plinth just standing there pointing. What at? Most of the tour guides along Las Ramblas will tell you he's pointing in the direction of America as if to say, 'Look, that's the place I'm about to discover.' Unfortunately that's not correct. He's pointing towards North Africa. So either Columbus's navigational skills were truly terrible or he's pointing at something else. Maybe he's pointing to the thief standing behind you. I prefer that one. 'Look out!' Chris is saying. 'Your purse is unzipped.'

The next day I'm on the Ramblas. It's going to be hard to make progress unless I come up with a plan but I have an idea. There is one group of street criminals in Barcelona that is a bit easier to spot than thieves. Easier to spot because they're selling something. They are the Three-Card Monte gangs and you can find them in many of Europe's big cities.

I saw Three-Card Monte on the streets of Nawlins but that guy was only playing. I'm on the lookout for the kind of guys who do it for real. The sort that play by entirely different rules and don't work alone.

Sure enough, halfway down the Ramblas, there's a game in full swing.

I can recognise this as Three-Card Monte right away. The dealer is a big guy, over six foot, dark biker jacket with jeans and a big strong East European nose on him that could rudder a tall ship. Playing with him is a group. It's a classic set-up.

Many potential players when they see a game of Three-Card Monte will watch for a while before they play. If there's a bit of a crowd, you can get a sense of the game and the dealer's technique by watching a few hands play out. Watch for a while and you will see some people win. And after another while you can see that the winners are the ones who seem to be paying closer attention. Monkey watches, monkey does. Armed with this confidence you decide that you've spotted the trick and you can follow the dealer's hand as he mixes the cards. You're going to win. So you play.

The problem is that the people you just saw playing – at least any of them who won a hand – are working with the dealer. Always. Every time. Every dealer has a gang of helpers who are called shills. Even though they're pretending not to know each other, passing real money around every time they 'win' or 'lose', the fact is that they are acting. They are putting on a show that they've put on a million times before with the sole intention of making it look easy to others.

This dealer has four shills. One is a middle-aged well-dressed woman (nobody is going to suspect her of being in a criminal gang), an old guy (probably been playing this game for forty years) and two younger, hip guys (backup in case things get physical).

In this dealer's version of the game he's using a fold-away mat instead of the cardboard box and shuffling three upside down matchboxes, under one of which is a white pea. The game moves quickly. He calls out to the crowd, 'Watch the pea, watch the pea.' He lifts one of the boxes to reveal the pea and then he quickly shuffles them around to mix them up. One of the crowd places a bet, fifty euros, and selects the upturned box on the right. The dealer lifts the box to reveal – wait for it – the pea! Hooray! Everyone claps. The dealer hold his hands out plaintively (all part of the act) and then gives a little round of applause to the player. 'Winner!' he cries and then he hands over a hundred euros to the player and deals again.

I'd bet two hundred euros that the player who just won is a shill.

Let's say you've missed that the people playing are shills. Let's say you've been sucked in and now you're interested in playing the game. The trickery doesn't stop there.

I can see that the dealer has spotted me but his glance doesn't dwell on me. He just repeats the game. This time he moves the boxes more slowly. He is letting me see that the pea is under the middle of the three boxes. All at once one of the other people standing around jumps in and (stupidly) picks the box on the left. The dealer lifts it to reveal no pea. The crowd groans. What a chump. It was obviously under the middle one. The dealer lifts the middle one to reveal what we could all see. If only that had been me. I could have won the hundred euros. Which is exactly what I'm meant to think.

The dealer wants me to think that I have the measure of him so I'll play next time. The problem is that he has another trick waiting. Another trick used in all Three-Card Monte games, whether it's a card or a matchbox. It goes like this. The dealer picks up one of the cards or boxes in, let's say the left hand, and two in the right. Now pay attention or you'll miss it.

He places the pea in one of the boxes in his right hand and throws it face down on the table. My eye automatically tricks me into believing that he's thrown the bottom one, the one containing the pea. But he hasn't. Using a bit of sleight of hand, he has actually thrown the uppermost box down first, which has no pea.

His plan is that even before I start trying to keep up with what happens next, I've already gone wrong. If I start wrong then how the hell am I going to end up anything but wrong?

The dealer is dealing again. This time, when the dealer stops, he looks directly at me. He draws me in. If this was a straight table and I could trust my eyes then I'd swear blind that the pea is under the middle box. One of the crowd, the guy who won the hundred euros earlier, smiles at me and nods, encouraging me to trust my instinct. 'The middle one,' he says with more friendly nods.

Let's say by some fluke I randomly by chance accidentally through no skill or judgement of my own, ended up picking the right box. What then? Surely then I would win?

Think again.

'Which one you think?' The dealer asks me straight. I can pick up an Eastern European accent in his voice. I step in closer. I'm close enough to see that a couple of his teeth are broken and the veins on his nose are prominent and ruddy. I pull a twenty-euro note from my pocket and move forward. 'No!' he cries. 'Fifty euro minimum.' I want to get in with this guy so I figure it's worth the investment. The only thing I know is that it's not under the middle box, so I decide to have a little fun with him.

I slap down my fifty. I'm meant to pick the centre box but instead I pick the box on the right. He pauses momentarily and fixes me a look. I can see him wondering what I'm up to. Either I'm stupid or I'm trying to play him. He affords me a little smile. But out of nowhere, up steps one of the shills and outbids me. He slaps the hundred-euro note down and pushes mine aside. Before I can protest, the dealer reveals it to be the right choice. But the shill wins. Highest bet takes all. Them's the rules.

Whatever bet you place, even if you fluke the right choice, one of the shills will always jump in and outbid you. You throw down your twenty euros but they'll jump in with a fifty or you'll have a fifty and they'll jump in with a hundred. They'll do it quickly and the dealer will not hesitate in revealing that it was the right choice and pay out accordingly. However aggrieved you might feel, the dealer will swear blind that the rule is he has to accept the highest bid, and only one bid at a time. You're close. But no cigar.

Against a team of shills and a dodgy dealer, you can never win.

But that doesn't mean it can't be fun to play. A good dealer and shills can make you feel like you're having a great time, even as you lose your money. They might sneakily let you win a hand but only to encourage you to bet higher stakes. In the end, you will lose.

One of the shills gives a loud shout and the dealer looks up towards where a couple of cops have appeared. No more time for messing around. He folds up the board and squirrels the matchboxes away into his pocket. An instant later he, and his shills, run off into the crowd. I try to follow them but they disappear in the throng and I'm left standing alone in the middle of the busy Ramblas again.

It's another couple of days before I see the dealer again. Would you believe it? He's surrounded by exactly the same players as last time. Different outfits but unmistakably the same faces. I stand a safe distance away and watch the game. He and his shills dance their familiar dance; they all know the steps by heart. His eyes flick up and down the street to see who is watching. He spots me and I see from his face that he recognises me.

From further away it is easier to see the trick much more clearly. The movement of the shills and the sleight of hand of the dealer are more obvious with some perspective. Usually when a player, or a mark, begins to play, the other shills will gather around pushing them closer to the game. It serves two purposes. First it shields the game from nosy onlookers who would be able to see the deceit from afar. Second, the closer the mark is to the dealer, the harder it is for him to spot the sleight of hand.

I continue to watch them play for a while and enjoy how they work a couple of marks. First a tourist couple who watch a few hands before the woman decides to throw down a fifty. She does it before her husband can stop her. Of course she loses. But she's determined and she throws down another fifty, despite her husband's protests. Same result. Before she can repeat this (and she does try), her husband picks her up off the ground and physically carries her away. The crowd laugh at the pantomime of it but I can see the dealer's a bit annoyed he didn't get the chance to milk her for more. As he's resetting the board, a couple of big thickset guys in leather jackets approach him. They don't look like the kind of guys you usually see playing Monte.

One of the guys has a shaven head and a nose that looks like it's been broken more times than a politician's promises. He says something to the dealer in what I guess is Russian, which seems to really piss the dealer off because a second later punches begin flying in from all angles. The big guy's nose takes a heavy right hook from the dealer, two of the guys who were 'betting' a minute before are now piling in, pushing, shoving and punching. Even the old lady weighs in with her pointy size fives directed to the back of the other big guy's knee.

If I needed any more proof that the shills and the dealer were working together then there it is. The Russians retreat and the gang move off together, keeping close, heading away from the Ramblas. I follow them in hot pursuit down a side street, determined not to lose them again. I catch up with them a couple of blocks away next to a small children's playground where they've stopped to regroup. With passions running high this isn't maybe the ideal time to make friends but it might be the best chance I get.

I approach tentatively. They're still clearly worked up from the fight. 'Hey, you guys okay?' I ask.

This is one of those heart pumping, hair sticking up on the back of your neck moments when you have no idea what is going to happen next. I can see that the dealer is trying to place me. One of his knuckles is bleeding slightly. 'We're not playing now. Come back later.'

'I saw what happened,' I say. 'Were they trying to muscle in?'

'Fucking Russians,' he says. 'But it's not a problem.'

I hold out my hand to shake his. 'I lost some money playing yesterday. But don't worry, that's not why I'm here. Can I buy you a beer?' I point to the store a couple of doors down.

'Sure. Why not?' He shrugs. 'You can always buy me a beer.'

We sit outside the local church with a couple of cans of Spanish beer from a convenience store. The dealer introduces himself as Michael and gives me a brown paper bag to put my beer in. I look at him unsure for a moment. 'In a bag, yes, yes, look.' He shows me how to do it as he hides his can in a bag. 'Now, police cannot judge me. I know, everybody knows. But they cannot judge you when you have it this way.'

And so it is that I find myself sitting like a street wino on the steps of a church chugging fizzy cold beer with Michael, a Three-Card-Monte dealer, from Kosovo.

Michael tells me he fled the former Yugoslavia during the war years in the early nineties. He's now nearly fifty years old and has spent the last twenty years travelling Europe conning tourists at the Three-Card Monte game. After another beer or two he begins to reminisce about what he calls the glory days in nineties Germany when he could make tens of thousands of Deutschmarks in a good day on the streets of West Berlin. So where is the money now? He points to his nose. Cocaine. 'You've put tens of thousands of dollars up your nose?' I ask.

'Hundreds.' He laughs. 'I've put a million dollars up my nose.'

Now he says business isn't quite so lucrative, which I guess is good news for his nose. He estimates that a good season, which is April to October, could net him somewhere between twenty and thirty thousand euros after he's paid the rest of the gang and the frequent fines he gets from Barcelona's police. He says it makes the difference between a trip back home to see his family or not. 'Thirty thousand. Then I go home,' he says. 'Twenty thousand, I must stay here until next year again.'

Michael says he learned the game out of desperation. He was often hungry back in Soviet times. 'You learn it very easily. When you are very hungry you learn everything.' Then he fixes me a look. 'You understand hungry?'

I don't think I understand it the way he means it. And I don't know what it feels like to be so hungry that it means you have to go out and fight Russians in the street. I ask him if he would show me how exactly he does the Three-Card Monte.

Michael's trick is a little different to others I've seen. He uses upturned matchboxes and the player has to find the pea. But when he gives me a demonstration I start to see what is happening. Michael is a magician. He shows you the pea under one box and then he shuffles. But, and I only see this when he slows it right down for me, while he's shuffling the boxes, he actually hides the pea in the small of his palm. He only returns it to a box after you've chosen. So there is absolutely no way you can ever win because the pea is in his hand until after you've bet. But he's so skilful at it that you'll never see that for yourself. David Blaine, eat your heart out.

Michael says that his dream is to work next year in Dublin. 'One year and I am king there, man. I can take too much money. I can take one, two thousand euro every day.'

Why is he so confident?

'Dublin people like to drink and they like to gamble,' says Michael. 'And I like to drink and to gamble. It's the same.'

'You'll be fine in Dublin, Michael,' I tell him. 'I don't worry about you at all. You'll be okay.'

Just then a younger guy in his early twenties in a cool jacket and shiny new trainers comes up to us. He shakes Michael's hand while looking at me. He asks Michael who I am. He addresses all his questions to Michael. Michael explains that I've been asking him questions about his life on the streets. The kid lights a cigarette. 'Yeah?' he says. This time he's looking at me. 'You want to know about life on the street, you should talk to me. I'm a pickpocket.'

'My name's Danny,' he says, finally shaking my hand.

I meet Danny again down a quiet residential street in a nice suburban district. He's got the same Letterman jacket and jeans on that he was wearing the day before, when I met him with Michael. I imagine this is his 'Sunday best', or his thief's uniform if you prefer. Danny's as keen as a puppy, giddy with excitement that I'm visiting him. Maybe he doesn't get many visitors. Maybe he's just going to rob me.

At the door to a neat-looking low-rise block of apartments, Danny stops and lets us inside. I follow him into the elevator and then down the hall to his apartment.

The first thing I notice is that there's a large crucifix hanging above the door. Christ, the Redeemer. Danny, the man needing redemption.

To my surprise, Danny lives with his whole family. His brother, mother, uncle and two nephews all share this two-bedroom apartment. They're a pasty bunch of chainsmokers but hospitable. Danny's mum even offers me one of her cigarettes. No thanks. Danny, his uncle and I sit down at the kitchen table and while everyone smokes another six fags, Danny's mum makes everyone a cup of tea.

I'm unsure at first whether Danny has entirely under-stood what I want to talk to him about. No kid is going to be comfortable speaking about the kind of 'profession' Danny has in front of his mother. If I was up to the kind of no good that Danny is, then my mum would give me a clip around the ear. I suggest to Danny maybe we need to find somewhere more private to have our chat. You know. Because your mum is here.

Danny laughs and translates for his mother. She lights up a cigarette and then laughs too.

'It's fine,' says Danny. 'She is a thief also.'

His mother nods enthusiastically through the fog of smoke. He says his mum has robbed more than all of them. From shops, mostly.

'But now that she is older she is retired. Now it's just me and him.' He's pointing to his uncle, a dead ringer for Fredo from the *Godfather* films. Fredo smiles, shrugs and lights up another cigarette.

Danny is very open about his work. He grew up in Romania where he spent two years in jail as a teenager for stealing a phone. He's quick to point out that for the same offence here in Spain he'd have received a sentence of three days. 'Three days sleeping, without smoke or alcohol,' he says. 'So is good. It is good to clean the body.'

He is speaking from experience. He's been caught stealing in Barcelona fourteen times. And fourteen times he has been sentenced to three days in a detention centre. Never any longer. He laughs at the system. 'Because it's like this, everybody comes here to steal.'

Danny lists off the other gangs he knows in Barcelona. He says there are Moroccans, Pakistanis, Arabs, Albanians, Italians. He raises an eyebrow and points at me. 'And Spaniards now, too. Even now they also steal. Now they don't have jobs, they steal.'

Spain has one of the highest youth unemployment rates in Europe. Approximately half of Spaniards under thirty have no regular job and live at home with their parents. Faced with so little opportunity, and maybe witnessing how well immigrant criminals like Danny are doing, it seems many have chosen to get in on the act.

The way Danny tells it, the gangs leave each other alone. He says there's plenty of work and no need for them to fight over territory. In any case, they all know the best places are the Ramblas and the metro and it doesn't pay to stand still. Pickpockets are always on the move circulating around the same areas and just quietly keeping out of each other's way. 'There is honour between thieves,' says Danny without a hint of irony.

It's not just with the other gangs that Danny is keen to avoid confrontation. His rule is never to steal from a Spaniard. 'I do not steal from them because it can get me in trouble. They can take us to the judge. Tourists no, they will leave the country anyway, so it is fine.'

It's a logical move. Not only do tourists typically carry wads of cash but they are also much less likely to give up their precious vacation to chase the police for a conviction. Especially the ones who can't speak Spanish.

Danny says the ideal targets are Asian tourists. He says they're 'hopelessly innocent' of the dangers that await them. The top three safest cities in the world, according to a recent report by *The Economist*, are all in Asia – Tokyo, Singapore and Osaka – and visitors from these places are often simply unaware that other parts of the world don't share their values, which sadly means they become good targets. 'They carry a lot of cash with them,' Danny says. 'And if they catch you, they just walk on. Never trouble.'

It shocks me that Danny is so brazen about racial profiling. But then maybe he's simply a hunter who has identified a trait that, more often than not, belies weakness. Like a lion who can see that a zebra is an easier kill than a buffalo. Especially a zebra with a brand-new Nikon camera sitting in his backpack.

I'm suddenly aware that I'm having a cup of tea with a real thief and his mum. He seems to have an agenda. He wants to be seen as the poor immigrant who, in the pursuit of wealth and status and with no other opportunities, has fallen prey to a life of crime. Someone who in the face of such adversity is still succeeding by being streetwise and hard-working. Told from Danny's perspective he is the victim, a victim of cruel circumstance.

I'm keen to see Danny in action. But I want to get up close and see it in all its gory detail. I ask him if he would take me out with him the next day. Maybe let me be part of the gang. He shakes his head. 'This is something that comes from family,' he says. 'It is in the blood.' He bangs his heart with his fist. And then points at me. 'You can't be a pickpocket because you have fear. But I am one. This is my job because I have no fear. Even to die.' And then he tells me that he's Robin Hood.

But didn't Robin Hood steal from the rich to give to the poor? This is often the mantra of the thief and I don't buy it for one second. Danny remains steadfast. 'We pick pockets and when we see a person in need then we give them money to buy food.'

I hear him say the words. But like I said, I don't believe it.

But I smile along anyway because I want him to show me how he works. After a bit more persuasion, he eventually acquiesces. I can come. I can watch. But don't get in the way or we'll all get arrested. That's fine with me. What's the worst that can happen anyway, I ask? We spend three days in detox?

Next day I'm waiting for Danny at the agreed rendezvous, down a quiet street just off the Ramblas. He's brought uncle Fredo and a friend called Chris. Chris is a dead ringer for a young Robert De Niro. Think *Once Upon a Time in America*. Is it just me or do all these guys actually look like movie stars? Chris has a bygone charm about him, good-looking and sharply dressed.

We discuss strategy. Uncle Fredo is going to run interference. That means his job is to walk at the shoulder of potential victims, screening their view from what is happening behind. Danny is the 'nudge' so when the time is right, he'll bump into the victim and throw them slightly off balance to provide the necessary distraction for Chris. Chris is the 'lift' and it's his job to actually pull the phone or wallet out of the victim's pocket or purse. Me? My job is to stay out of everyone else's way.

With that settled, I set off on one of the more unusual

Saturday afternoons of my life so far – pickpocketing with a gang of Romanian thieves.

Last night I had imagined the way that today would pan out. We'd pick an area. We'd case the angles to work out where the best spot was for a theft. We'd wait patiently for the perfect victim to come along. Then we'd strike and put our meticulously worked strategy into play. The result would be the perfect seamless crime.

What actually happens is nothing like that.

Within seconds of passing through the barriers to the metro, the boys are at work. They spot a couple of male Asian-looking tourists and Fredo immediately falls into step at their shoulder. Danny pushes in close throwing them slightly off balance as Chris, bold as brass, begins to unzip one of the boys' backpacks. I can see that the boy has noticed. It looks like maybe he felt something but as he goes to turn around, Danny barges into him, which creates enough distraction for Chris to get his whole hand into the bag.

I am astonished. Partly at the sheer brazenness of the act but also at the speed with which it happens. Chris pulls his hand out of the bag but it is empty. He turns to me with a shrug. Nothing worth stealing. But he doesn't look disappointed. We jump onto the metro train for one stop and then we're off again towards the exit.

As we reach the steps to the exit, the boys spot a potential victim, and fall into position again. This time it's a girl on her own. As she is climbing the steps, her bag bobs up and down on her hip. Danny doesn't even need to bump past her this time as her own motion up the steps is creating enough distraction for Chris to do his bit. His dexterity is beyond belief. I watch as his long nimble fingers slowly unzip the bag and then dip in and pull out the girl's purse. Chris hands off the purse to Danny and then seconds later, at the top of the steps, Danny hands me the purse. He has already opened it to show me that it contains a bundle of euros and a couple of credit cards. I take the purse and suddenly it dawns on me that I have committed a crime. An accomplice to an assault on another innocent human being.

I can't lie, the whole experience was thrilling. My heart is racing. The adrenaline began flowing the second I realised we were doing something wrong and that we could get caught. In the moment that Chris's hand was inside the girl's purse, I was focused solely on the prize, performing my job as lookout, willing him on to success. I am guilty of behaving recklessly and without consideration of the consequences for anyone, including myself and certainly not the girl.

The girl. It hits me like a train. I must catch up with the girl. I leave Danny and Chris standing and run after the girl to hand back her purse. I have to tap her on the shoulder to get her attention and I'm struck by how defensive she is as she turns around. She clutches her bag to herself as though she fears I might be about to rob her. I can't help but notice the irony. I hold out her purse. It takes her a second to realise what it is before she snatches it out of my hand. I apologise profusely and clumsily try to explain to her that I mean her no harm. I am still shaking from all the adrenaline.

The girl is Spanish. And furious. It takes twenty minutes to persuade her not to go to the cops. My explanation of what I am doing and why I am doing it doesn't make any sense to her. Danny and Chris stand by, watching, smoking cigarettes and seem just to find the whole thing funny. Eventually, girl placated, they simply shrug, their indifference made clear, and then they go back to work.

I wonder how important the team is for Danny's operation. 'Yes. This is the most important. I can't do it by myself. In the metro, for example, it is impossible. Without a team you can't do it. And if you don't want to go to the prison you have to have a good team.'

And if one gets caught, do they all get punished?

'Yes. Of course.'

Back in the metro Danny and Chris target another and then another tourist. Each time I insist we return whatever valuable item they have taken: a phone, a wallet, a purse and even a pair of reading glasses. It seems effortless to them. Anyone they choose is vulnerable to their skills and within an hour and a half they've stolen (and I've returned) enough to pay the rent.

As we board the next train, I'm starting to think this is all too easy, when a man in his mid-thirties, dressed in casual black coat and jeans, stops and orders us to stay where we are. Slightly affronted, I ask him who he is but when he lifts up his coat to show me his gun and a set of handcuffs tucked into his belt, I quickly shut up. We've been busted. I immediately start to worry about what's going to happen to us. I'm thinking about the girl at the top of the steps. Did she go to the cops after all? I wouldn't blame her. I'm kicking myself for not calling this a day much sooner. I'm guilty of being involved in this crime and I'm guilty of being seduced by the artistry of the two young men. I look over to them to see if they are worried but they are giggling at some private joke. I give Danny a 'WTF?' look but he just shrugs and shakes his head. He seems totally relaxed. At the next station the police officer ushers us off the train.

On the platform, I try to explain to the cop what is going on. I assure him that this is a demonstration and that anything that the boys have 'stolen' has been immediately returned to the victim. He looks at me in total disbelief. 'Do you know who these guys are?' he asks. 'These guys are thieves. They steal every day. This one.' He points at Danny. 'This one is probably the most famous thief in Barcelona.' I look at Danny. He seems almost proud of the moniker until the cop adds, 'Not because he's the best, because he's been caught so many times. Every cop in Barcelona knows his face now.'

With nothing to hold us on, the cop eventually lets us go with a warning. He makes me promise to leave the metro and finish our exercise. If not, then he will arrest me. Danny seems a little agitated by the interruption and becomes grumpy. He asks me if I've seen enough. He says he doesn't care about the police and that Chris is tired of showing off for no money. Because I keep insisting that we hand stuff back to the victims, I'm bad for business and now the whole exercise has lost its novelty value.

I ask Danny about what the cop said. He laughs it off and tells me the cop knows about only a fraction of what he does. I wonder why it is that Danny thinks he is so good at pickpocketing. Why be a pickpocket in the first place? He says he remembers once, as a kid, he saw a lot of money and he liked it.

'If you work you're going to make money little by little, but if you pickpocket you can make lots of money at once.'

Which explains the motivation but not the talent.

'I think is not a "talent" but the fact that I look like normal, just as anybody else,' he explains. 'People don't look at me different, they are not scared about me. I am always wearing nice clothes so they can't figure out that I am a pickpocket.'

For Danny the hard bit is not the dexterity but the disguise. He needs to look like everybody else and after that, he just needs courage.

I wonder if he is happy.

'Yes. Sadness has gone and now I am happy. When my family is well I am happy and if I have what I want to eat and to drink and a bed to sleep and sometimes marijuana then all is fine.' He turns away from me, saying, almost under his breath, that he would love to have a respectable well-paid job like I have but he doesn't look as though he really means it. 'Any work I am offered I would do. I don't have a real profession. You think my profession is pickpocket? No. If I find a job as waiter or manual labour I don't mind, I would do anything.'

'But is that what you want to do?' I ask. 'What do you think you would be best at?'

He smiles and shakes his head. 'No. For sure, what I do best is pickpocketing.'

He translates this last bit for Chris and they both laugh at his joke, which clearly isn't a joke. They high five each other and we all walk back along the street towards the Ramblas.

As we walk along the road, we pass other people. Danny walks up behind a girl and pinches her backside. She recoils in horror. Danny winks at me as though there's something cute about it. There isn't. Further along the road, he and Chris face down a couple of teenage boys much younger than them. Danny raises a fist and mocks to punch them before he laughs in their faces. The younger boys look terrified. I start to see another side to Danny and Chris. Not a very pleasant one.

I bid the boys goodbye when we reach the main street. As Chris shakes my hand he notices my watch and makes a joke (I think it's a joke) out of trying to slide it off my wrist. I have to pull my hand away quite forcefully. They roll their eyes at each other and then they disappear into the crowd. As they walk off I carefully check all my pockets until I'm confident that I still have my wallet and my passport. I turn around and quickly walk in the opposite direction.

CHAPTER FIVE

CANNABIS CAM

*'The market's good at the moment,
trust me, yeah, it's good'*

No LIST OF the world's greatest cities would be complete without including Birmingham. No offence to Alabama, but I'm talking about Birmingham, England. I'll admit to a bit of bias on this one, because Birmingham is the city where I grew up. I've decided that I can't really claim all these other cities are laden with crooks and villains without applying the same scrutiny a little closer to home. So I'm going back to investigate a silent crime epidemic that nobody seems to want to talk about.

Birmingham is no tourist town. It built its reputation on manufacturing during the Industrial Revolution. Once upon a time, it was a place you could be proud of when its heavy industry rivalled any in the world – the steam engine was invented here. But over the last thirty years, like many big Western cities where manufacturing has become a thing of the past, it has slowly developed into a service sector economy leading the world in public administration. Still, it's the second biggest city in the UK.

Birmingham isn't ever going to win any beauty contests either. During the Second World War, it paid a high price for being the powerhouse of British munitions production when the city took more than its fair share of German bombs. Look around today and you'll see a town rebuilt by post-war zealots who, seduced by brutalist ideology, saw concrete monoliths and high-rise tower blocks as the surest route to creating a socialist utopia. How wrong they were.

However, it has its charms and today, as the blue sky stands in sharp contrast to the grey concrete, I'm struck by what a great day it is in Birmingham. I make the trip north pretty often because my family still live here. But there's no time for a family BBQ on this occasion because I'm here to see a man about some dope.

Birmingham is by no means a crime hot spot. The two most common crimes according to its police force are anti-social behaviour and shoplifting, which is pretty standard for a big city, and crimes related to violence and drugs are in line with the national average.

But I'm en route to the house of a man who I know is a criminal. The address he's given me is in the more salubrious environs of Birmingham's green and leafy suburbs so I find myself walking among large detached houses with well-appointed gardens. This is where the people with money live. The rhododendrons and azaleas are in full bloom and the lawns have been meticulously manicured. It's regular middle-class suburbia. No sign of the kind of social malaise usually associated with urban crime. I have to double-check the address.

The front door opens and inside is a fair-haired young man who looks like he didn't eat enough of his greens growing up. I'd guess he's in his mid-twenties but he's not grown higher than your average twelve-year-old. Ben is a friend of a friend and has kindly invited me to his house to see the fruits of his gardening endeavours. The house he lives in is a big Victorian redbrick where Ben says he lives with his mother. He also tells me that presently his mother is out, which is why this is a particularly good time for me to come round. He's asked me to protect his identity for various reasons, the main one of which is that his mother doesn't know that he's growing cannabis. In her loft.

You might not have had a reefer since the days when people still called it a reefer but it seems pretty much everyone else is at it like Snoop Dogg. The Office for National Statistics estimates that around 2 million adults (7 per cent) in England and Wales smoked weed last year. I've also heard reasonable claims that the true figure is more than double that. Whoever you believe, what has changed beyond all recognition is where everyone is getting their weed from. Made in Britain is a rare label to see these days but, amazingly, it turns out that in the twenty-first century, there is one manufacturing industry that is in rude health. No surprise that Birmingham is a centre of excellence. Just don't tell the Germans.

Ben pops the hatch to the space beneath the roof and lowers a telescopic ladder. He climbs up and I follow him into the darkness above. He switches on a small lamp and I can immediately see that one corner of the ample loft space has been sectioned off with plastic sheeting. It reminds me of a quarantine tent like the ones the FBI use in the movies when they discover you're harbouring aliens.

Ben points at it. 'Inside there,' he says. Inside there, he is growing hydroponic cannabis.

Hydroponics was initially developed by the Dutch for the purpose of producing fruit and vegetables. Holland has a high population density and a relatively poor climate for cultivation, so they developed a system for growing plants indoors. The Dutch worked out that by controlling light, temperature, pH and CO_2, plants could be tricked into producing high yields of high quality. At first it was applied to fruit but it didn't take long before the cannabis industry took over and developed the technology to NASA space-laboratory level.

As we crawl across the loft space above Ben's mother's bedroom, I can also just make out a very faint mechanical hum that I couldn't hear from downstairs. We shuffle towards it on our hands and knees. Ben peels back the corner edge of the plastic and at once a bright orange glow floods the upper space. There is just room enough for us to crawl inside. Operation Control. Ben has two lights under which plants grow in trays full of nutrient solutions while an industrial-sized extractor fan recycles air through the chimney. The whole system, lighting and irrigation is automated by a bank of timers on the wall. It's pretty slick.

Cannabis growers fall into two categories. In the red corner there's the hobby growers: cannabis connoisseurs, habitual smokers, tight of purse and lip. They squirrel away half a dozen or so plants in a tight space somewhere in their houses (up to nine plants is generally regarded as the threshold for what the law regards as personal use). They justify what they do as in terms of quality assurance and avoiding 'real' criminals. Their grow rooms are high-tech and they haven't brought a girl (for they are mostly men) home for years for fear that she might disapprove or run off and tell the police.

Ben is a hobby grower. He has eight cannabis plants. He knows the rules. He doesn't want to risk being accused of being a dealer because if he gets caught that would likely mean a heavy sentence from the court. But as a hobby grower, Ben knows that he's likely to escape with a caution or, at worst, a fine. Unless his mum finds out, in which case it could be a lot worse.

My own feelings about cannabis are pretty ambivalent. I think there are more serious crimes for us to focus on. I also think that the criminalisation of cannabis is pretty hypocritical when judged against tobacco or alcohol, both of which seem to do as much harm. But mostly, as someone who likes to follow the money, I wonder if we aren't missing a huge opportunity for UK plc not to regulate it and make some much-needed extra tax dollars, like is already happening in the USA. But it's not up to me, so for now Ben's activities are still illegal.

Ironically, though, Ben says his main reason for getting into growing is that it takes him out of the criminal loop. He says that when you grow your own, then you don't have to meet up with the kind of criminals that sell it. 'I don't want to give my hard-earned cash to some kid on a push bike, selling ten bags that he's bought from some criminal who's probably also selling Class As,' he says. Self-sufficiency allows a way off the criminal grid.

I must admit I have some sympathy with this ambition. I'm essentially a libertarian and I subscribe to a view that says if you are an adult and what you're doing does not cause anyone else any harm and is happening in the privacy of your own home, then who are they to tell you not to do it? Someone growing their own cannabis for their own consumption as a way of keeping their habit to themselves and, in the process, not putting money into some criminal gang's hands sounds okay to me.

As we sit in his mum's loft under the warm glow of an artificial sun, Ben talks me through the different strains of cannabis he is cultivating. It could be a naughty edition of *Gardener's World*. There are cannabis plants from all over. There's one called Hindu Kush and another that he calls Lemon Kush (which does smell very citrony), there's the Northern Lights that he assures me gives a 'heavy stone' and another brand-new variety that he's created himself from crossing different strains. I have to admire the dedication to what I'll credit seems like a genuine hobby. Ben says that he was never creative at school and growing cannabis is something in which he takes an enormous pride. He has a respectable full-time job but cannabis is his recreational drug of choice when the working day is done. He never sells any of it because he is a regular enough smoker to get through it all. I don't ask what his full-time job is but I hope he's not a GP.

But people like Ben are only half the story. In the blue corner are the professional growers. These guys mean business. They have eschewed the rigorous methodology of the hobby growers and instead adopt a pack 'em high, sell 'em high, get 'em high approach to the commercial practice of getting people stoned.

About twenty years ago, seeing a gap in a growth market, East Asian gangs, mostly from China and Vietnam, started to move into the UK cannabis cultivation business. Police forces in big conurbations such as London, Liverpool and Birmingham which have sizeable

Asian diasporas, started reporting seizures of large quantities of fresh cannabis found in industrial-sized indoor grow rooms. These gangs knew how to grow well and they took over the market. They typically grew a thousand or more plants at a time.

The question of how much a cannabis plant is worth is a tricky one to answer. An ounce of weed sells for around two hundred pounds. Most commercial growers produce plants that contain 3.5 to 5 ounces (100–140 grams) of cannabis so we'll work to the conservative end of that range and say that a plant is worth seven hundred pounds (with the caveat that it could be up to 50 per cent more). Either way, the East Asian grow rooms that the police were busting were earning their bosses upwards of seven hundred thousand pounds every few months.

Ben admits there are times when his consumption outstrips his personal supply. During these dry weeks, he turns to other growers who have more than they need. He's given me the number of one of them who he says always has surplus because, unlike Ben, he grows more than he needs. Next to the number scribbled on the scrap of paper he hands me is the name: Vee.

Vee has agreed to meet me at a pub on the outskirts of Wolverhampton. If you thought Birmingham needed a facelift, then wait until you see its little sister, Wolverhampton. A concrete ring road of pound shops, pie shops and pawn shops. The pub where we've agreed to rendezvous is particularly nasty. The sign on the wall outside offers meals for £3.99, as if that is something to be proud of, and inside there's three Cross of St George flags tacked to the walls, which as far as I'm concerned has only one connotation in modern Britain. While I wait for Vee, I order a pint of beer. It's considerably warmer than the atmosphere in here. Any food? No thanks.

Vee texts to say he's waiting outside. Can't blame him for not wanting to come in. The car's running and I can see another guy sitting in the passenger seat, so I slide into the back. With only a cursory nod in my direction, he takes off. Vee is a drug dealer. He's a heavyset young Asian man who wears a lot of gold jewellery and casual sportswear. He looks like he's going to a fancy dress party as Ali G. Vee's customers are mainly based in Wolverhampton but he says he makes deliveries all over Birmingham. And that's what we're off to do together now.

The drug dealer is to many the soft end of the criminal world and the marijuana dealer is the soft end of the dealer world. A friend of mine described to me once how a guy she met on a date told her that in the past he'd served time in jail. Before he could tell her exactly what for, she found herself thinking 'Please let it be drugs. Please let it be drugs.' (Alas, it was Grievous Bodily Harm. Date over. She left.) But while cannabis dealing is a borderline socially acceptable criminal career these days, it's important to remember it does still have its downsides.

Driving around the environs of Wolverhampton, Vee gives me a potted history of his life so far, the highlight of which is that Vee served six years in jail for cannabis cultivation. It sounds like a long stretch for a guy who looks like he only recently started shaving, but the experience of prison doesn't seem to have put him off. Ten minutes into our drive, he pauses the storytelling to conduct an illegal financial transaction through the window of his car. The buyer is a smaller dealer who exchanges two hundred pounds for an ounce of cannabis. Seconds later we drive away. I wonder where Vee gets his cannabis from. He looks at me in the rear-view mirror. 'Grow it all myself.'

Vee currently has four cannabis 'farms' in production. He uses rented properties around town, all of which are located in what he describes as 'nice areas'. He sounds like an estate agent. Each farm is growing around a hundred plants that each produce three to five ounces of cannabis every three months. Add up those numbers and it means that Vee is grossing in the region of one hundred thousand pounds per annum from cannabis. He reasons that more farms is better because the important thing is to spread his risk. I wonder what the main risk is. Is Vee worried about going back to prison? 'Not really,' he says. 'That's not what I'm worried about.'

There is something much more troubling than the police to keep Vee up at night.

'There are some seriously nasty bastards out there,' he says. 'If they find out you've got a grow room somewhere, then they'll come looking.'

According to Vee, the Chinese have been squeezed out of the market. The proliferation of cannabis farms into smaller properties has squeezed the market but the side-effect is that some very unsavoury criminals have joined in. Not to grow but to exploit a lucrative sideline: robbing cannabis farms.

For a serious criminal with a record in armed robbery or worse, it's a safer bet to rob a cannabis farm than, say, the local post office because they know guys like Ben and Vee can't or won't go to the police. The unhealthy consequence of guys like Vee (small fish) taking over from the Chinese gangs is that it increases the risk of attracting the attention of other nastier criminals (sharks), who want to rob them. Which could become a problem for the rest of us if Vee sets up one of his farms on your street.

That night I pop in to visit my mum. The picture that's been painted by Ben and Vee suggests that in Britain today, the buds in your weekend spliff are likely to have been cultured, nurtured and harvested inside residential properties. Reasonable estimates have half a million people now growing cannabis in the UK, in which case, we could say, on average, there's a cannabis farm on almost every street. As I go to sleep I work out the odds that there's someone growing dope on my mum's street. There's a fair chance that someone round here is growing weed in their loft or basement or spare room or maybe all three.

The next day I put in a call to a friend who works for a local newspaper in Wolverhampton. I tell him what I've heard from Vee and ask him what he's heard locally about criminals targeting cannabis farms. He points me in the direction of some pieces he's filed from Birmingham Crown Court. The city has recently started to see more cases of just that – violent criminals using sophisticated techniques to locate where small-time growers are farming cannabis. Gangs have placed tracking devices on cars parked outside hydroponics shops and even trained their own drug dogs to sniff out grow rooms. It's a phenomenon known as 'taxing', and my friend says he might have a contact for me that I can talk to about it. The only downside is that we'll have to go to Handsworth to meet him.

Birmingham has nicer suburbs than Handsworth: for example, all of them. For a long time, it's been Birmingham's problem child. In the last twenty years it has hosted three sets of riots and trouble often spills over in the area as young black and Asian gang members fight over turf. It's only a couple of miles away from where I met Ben but it feels like another world entirely. Still, Handsworth is representative of much of Britain's poorest inner cities in that it is largely non-white, high unemployment rate, drug use is rife and crime rates are more than double the national average. It is the perfect environment for bad guys to operate.

The exact time and location for our meeting has been set for late afternoon at a small terraced house along a tatty street. When I step out of the car I have to admit I am a little intimidated by the choice. It's getting dark and I am in the heart of Handsworth where, even though I grew up less than five miles from here, or maybe because I did, I know not to walk around at night.

I push the bell and we're buzzed inside. The house has been divided into flats so I follow my contact through a communal hallway and up two flights of stairs. The wallpaper is yellow and peeling in places, the whole place smells musty and damp. The main room is bare but for two striking details. First, there is a large dark stain in the middle of the old carpet, which looks suspiciously like blood, and another hand-shaped stain on the far wall, which is definitely blood. Second, there is the man I have come to meet standing in the middle of the room dressed completely in black – trousers, shirt, coat, gloves and hat. Like he's going to a funeral.

Now I really need to be careful about protecting this guy's identity. Partly because he's asked me to but mainly because he's a convicted murderer. By which I mean he has served time in prison for it. So I'm taking his request very seriously. Let's just say he's a really big guy with arms and legs and a face and leave it at that. And we can call him Cam.

I never imagined when I was a schoolboy down the road from here that I would end up interviewing a murderer about his new-found interest in cannabis farms. In fact, when I was a schoolboy, I didn't even consider that there were murderers walking around these streets. But according to the Ministry of Justice, every year around three hundred people are locked up for murder in the UK and one to two hundred convicted murderers are also released from prison. There's a veritable revolving door of murderers passing in and out of the clinks. What do they do next? I'm about to find out.

I ask Cam how business is going. Like we're just two guys hanging out, talking about work. That's all. He nods and smiles. 'There's a lot of money out there. The market's good at the moment, trust me, yeah, it's good.'

Cam looks pretty content. We're off to a good start.

It's hard to be sure why Cam is here. Perhaps it is a favour to our mutual friend but I'm not convinced that would be enough of a draw. I think Cam wants to talk about his job. After a hard day in the office, which one of us doesn't like to come home and offload about the day we've had? Who doesn't like to be told that they're good at what they do or have someone be impressed by the problem they solved that nobody else could? We are all social creatures. We spend most hours of our days working. I think for guys like Cam, there's a frustration about life lived in the shadows. I imagine it can feel lonely and isolated. Even though what Cam does is criminal, it's still nice to be asked how your day was.

When he talks about the market, I wonder if he means small-time growers.

'Yeah. I don't know why but just bare people are growing, growing, growing, it used to be just a few people at one time but now everybody's sort of at it.'

Cam confirms that not only are more people than ever growing weed in Birmingham but that the old way of doing it in industrial units is on the wane.

The market is changing rapidly. This is one trade war that the Chinese are losing. Cam says that as more people favour smaller houses that 'don't arouse suspicion', he's constantly on the lookout for the telltale signs. 'You know, certain things like you look at the curtains and stuff, if they've never been drawn. Bin bags that ain't been put out so if somebody's supposed to be living there, why ain't there been no rubbish? You get me?' Cam says these are all signs that those houses aren't really being lived in.

It strikes me as a sign of the scale of the industry that someone like Cam can make his living not from growing cannabis but from stealing it.

He has a high level of scorn for those that are doing it too. 'They're just punks,' he says. 'Pussies, not real criminals.' He scoffs at these fly-by-night wannabes trying to turn a quick buck. Woe betide them if Cam comes knocking at the door.

The key, Cam says, is to make sure he knocks at the right time. Once he suspects a house has some cannabis growing inside it, he stakes it out to work out when the cannabis is ready to harvest. 'No point in hitting it at the wrong time,' explains Cam. 'You want it when the crop is full, then you can just cut it all down, take it away and sell it.'

Cam is no fool. He's thought about his MO. He has worked out the angles on how to conduct his business and from the sound of him, he takes his work very seriously.

What happens if the people who are growing the crop resist?

'You just deal with them. We just beat the shit out of them. Torture them if we have to. We'll torture really cos you want to know where else they might be growing or where they've hidden the money.'

Cam is so matter of fact that he could be a plumber explaining to me what he has to do to unblock a drain. He talks with the happy confidence of a man chatting about his work. He's on comfortable ground. As I realise this, I see that nothing he is saying shocks him.

Maybe he's just done it so many times it doesn't register any more.'

I suddenly have an image of Cam coming crashing through my door or the door of one of my family members, and I wonder what the hell being tortured by Cam is like.

He carries on with his explanation. 'We take claw hammers, machetes, ropes and duct tape.' Cam is in free flow now. 'Sometimes they're not growing there but you know they're growing somewhere else so you need to get that information.'

Now suddenly this is an even bigger problem. Because what if you're genuinely not growing anything? What if your neighbour is the grower but Cam has come through your door by mistake? And what if, despite your protestations, he doesn't believe your story? Cam doesn't seem like the kind of guy who says, 'Oh, sorry. Wrong house. I'll try next door.'

'You don't really want to like go OTT on them because at the end of the day you just want the information.' He's stone cold. 'Just give them a good beating on the legs, you know what I mean? Or across the ribs, hammers on their feet and their toes and stuff, whack them a few times with hammers on there, they'll soon start talking. If that don't work then I have the sun bed and sparky.'

The sun bed? Sparky?

Cam has a sun bed. In a garage in Birmingham. Which he takes people to. Which he duct tapes people into. Which he leaves on. Until they talk. 'Man needs to be careful not to leave it on too long though yeah?' he says almost chuckling at the idea. 'Or you can burn a man bad. That happened once.'

Cam also has a box. Which he calls sparky. It's a high-voltage battery with wires coming out of it. 'You just hook it up and you can use it to get information out of a man.' Apparently, that works well. 'Quickly. I know it sounds bad but you just have to go in there, get your information, get out there and just move on as quickly as possible. We ain't in there to make friends.'

He's right. It does sound bad.

I have a clear image in my head of Ben, the charming young hobby grower, and his mum oblivious to the cannabis being grown in her loft. I have an image of them tied up with duct tape while Cam electrocutes them for the information he 'needs'. I shudder at the thought of the pain and suffering that Cam would inflict upon them both before he made off with Ben's prize-winning Lemon Kush. It doesn't bear thinking about how Ben and his mother would ever recover from such an experience.

Using these dastardly techniques, Cam says a 'usual' haul is around four kilos. This is what the new small house model is typically responsible for. Four kilos of good-quality cannabis should change hands for upwards of twenty thousand pounds but Cam says he takes a dis-count from his buyer for fast cash. All in all he says he's happy with fifteen thousand pounds for a job.

'Do you enjoy your job?' I ask Cam.

He takes a moment to properly consider this question before he answers.

'Not really, I wouldn't say really I enjoy my job, it's something that I've gotta do. Everybody's smoking it, what can you do? I'm just gonna reap it in while I can, until something changes.'

And what could change to make him stop?

'They might just fucking legalise it tomorrow and man, when a man can grow it legally, that's gonna be the end of that.'

'So legalisation would put you out of work?'

'Put me out of work, prohibition style.'

I shake Cam's hand and thank him for his time. It's a strange feeling to behave with such social nicety towards a man who has just confessed such gruesome acts to me with casual indifference. But what else can I do? He's been respectful, considerate of my questions and he's asked for nothing in return. I'm genuinely grateful.

Back outside the thought won't leave me that cannabis legalisation isn't going to happen any time soon around here. So I think again about the cruel irony that people like Ben get into growing cannabis so as to avoid coming into contact with small-time criminals but actually risk running into much bigger-time ones like Cam instead. My initial libertarian feelings towards cannabis cultivation have been turned on their head because it's suddenly harder to see it as such a victimless activity when there's maniacs like Cam running around.

Because where does it end? What if it was my door getting kicked in by Cam? What if he mistakenly thought that I was growing cannabis? Maybe the bloke next door has forgotten to take the bins out. Maybe I was away on holiday last week, left the curtains drawn, and Cam has jumped to the wrong conclusion. Either way, it may take a long sun-bed session before I could reassure him that he's made a mistake.

I feel like it's not cool to be down on cannabis in the UK any more. In the UK, the commonly held perception seems to be that as cannabis is so ubiquitous, we should all just learn to relax about it. Before I met Cam, I probably subscribed to that view too but now that I have met him, I can't help but feel worried for my family who live only a few miles away from this monster. I'm worried for everyone that lives in a community where Cam lives too.

Cannabis might be more prevalent than ever before in Western society but while it retains any degree of illegality then it creates an environment in which bad men can operate with abandon. That alone should be reason enough to change the law. It certainly needs to be talked about more openly in any case.

And what about the other thousands of serious criminals out there? Cam says that he operates alone. He is not part of any gang. This strikes me as unusual. I had hitherto always thought that guys like Cam worked with accomplices. Maybe it's only a matter of time before he gets more organised.

For most of us, the idea of being kidnapped and tortured is our worst nightmare. I was interested to find out more about the kind of men who engage in kidnap and in particular those who prey, not on naughty cannabis growers, but on those who are completely innocent.

CHAPTER SIX
SANTA MUERTE

'If I take you, you'll be safe'

HOLY DEATH IS her name. In Mexico she is revered as a folklore saint, depicted as a crowned skeleton in a long flowing robe, globe in one hand and scythe in the other. They say that when you die, she will meet you at the banks of the Styx to judge you and, if you're in favour, will clear your path to the next life. So until then, it's probably worth staying on her good side.

Much to the chagrin of the Catholic Church, Holy Death, or Santa Muerte in Spanish, is more popular than ever. Millions of Mexicans worship her and make offerings to her idols in search of better fortune. The church can condemn her all they like, but Santa Muerte is very 'in' right now.

Devotion to Holy Death is what anthropologists call a 'cult of crisis'. She draws devotees from the poorer parts of society. The prostitutes and the thieves, the homosexuals and the drug addicts, the dealers and the gangsters all venerate her. They have plumped for a champion who understands them. Many will talk of how Santa Muerte is the sole resident of heaven to understand the violence and struggles that are part of their everyday life.

Another curious association is that Santa Muerte is the patron saint of taxi drivers in Mexico. I've been many a place whose taxi drivers (and their passengers) were more in need of divine intervention – Delhi, Cairo, Hanoi to name a few – but here in Mexico City, taxi drivers will often hang a figurine of her from the rear-view mirror. They say it is to bring them protection from being robbed. But from what I've heard about Mexico City's taxis, it's the customers who need the protection.

Secuestro express translates as express kidnap. It's a hit-and-run kind of kidnap where you're kidnapped, robbed and still home in time for tea. The way it works is like this. Prime time to be hit for a secuestro express is around 11 p.m. when you're happily stumbling home after dinner with a few drinks inside you. You hail a cab, a car pulls up, you jump in, and before you know it, you're being held at gunpoint and driven to the nearest ATM. They like to strike just before midnight because that's when most people's daily ATM withdrawal limit resets. So the robber can get five hundred dollars this side of the clock and another five hundred the other side. Done right, it only takes a few minutes. You're back on the sidewalk, down a thousand dollars and still looking for a cab.

The way the local press tell it, secuestro express is reaching epidemic proportions in Mexico City. Residents have been complaining that the police are not doing enough about it, which is having a negative impact on the city's reputation. Allegations of corruption at the highest levels abound. But then that's true for many of Mexico's social problems.

Mexico City's crime index is high. But so what? That's true for many big cities. You're still twice as likely to be murdered in Washington DC, and five times more likely in New Orleans. Nor are robbery rates in Mexico City very different to London or Paris. And, in terms of the rest of the country, crime in the capital is much lower than places like Colima or Guerrero.

But what is unique about Mexico City is the prevalence of the secuestro express. It's the main reason for my fascination with it. I want to see if I can penetrate the world of secuestro express and even meet some of the people behind it.

I've decided the best way to do that is to jump straight in.

Until now I've used taxis as a way into other criminal worlds. In Buenos Aires they were a route to the counterfeiting gangs and in Mumbai, well, let's not ever talk about Mumbai again. But it works. Of course, now in Mexico, there's a new frisson because it's the taxi driver himself that I suspect of being involved in the serious crime. It gives a whole new perspective to taking a cab here.

The first taxi I hail seems pretty standard. The driver is smartly dressed. He's mid-forties, wearing a smart shirt and a chunky gold watch. What's unusual is that he hands me his ID card and laminated credentials from the City of Mexico that prove he's a licensed cab. Before I say anything, he reassures me that no kidnap is going to happen because he's a Segundo (a safe taxi) but for that, the fare will be a hundred pesos instead of the usual thirty. Why so much more? I ask. 'You pay extra for a safe taxi,' he says.

If you needed a clear indication that the situation here has got out of hand, then there it is, you have to consent to being ripped off if you want an assurance you won't be robbed. Screwed if you do, screwed if you don't.

My taxi drops me at the Ciudadela Market. It's a typical tourist market: hundreds of stalls selling traditional arts and crafts strung along a busy street. The crowds pass in both directions, gawping at the array of tourist tat. It's what the Mexicans call Artezanía – clay pots depicting pre-Hispanic gods, gaudy, orange palm-fibre baskets and miniature musical instruments. Tiny ukulele, anyone? The kind of stuff you instantly regret buying as soon as you open the suitcase back home.

On the far side of the square I can see a bit of a crowd. There's music playing and it sounds like there's a party going on, so I walk over to check it out. It's got to be more fun than the market. The first thing I notice is that people are dancing. Proper dancing. People of all ages, young and old, are twirling each other around to a salsa beat. Some of the older ones are dressed up like Minnie the Moocher in zoot suits and wide-brimmed fedora hats. The women too are dolled up to the nines in slinky dresses and heels like stilts.

Before I know it a guy who can't be an inch over four foot six, wearing a purple pinstriped suit and a black hat tipped over one eye, pulls my arm and calls me to join in. He grabs the nearest woman and together they give me a short demonstration. Some of the coolest and sexiest dancing I've ever seen. What this guy lacks in height he more than makes up for in style. With a final flourish, he spins his partner around, slides her down his left arm and presents her to me like he's offering me the second half of a burger he's not sure he wants any more.

I can't dance like that. But thankfully, she knows what she's doing enough to avoid my clumsy size nines. We do a passing impression of Ginger Rogers and a baby elephant until the song finishes and we even get a little applause from the crowd who have gathered round to see whether the Gringo can dance. My little friend seems pleased so he pulls me over to the bar for a shot of tequila. His Spanish is spoken with a heavy slang but I'm pretty sure the gist of it is, What the hell are you doing round here?

I tell him that I'm in town looking to find out about secuestro express. I want to meet some of the people involved in it. He looks me up and down again. 'Are you serious?' I nod. He shrugs and orders up two more tequilas like we're going to need them.

'These are bad people you're talking about,' he says. 'You don't want to mess around in that world or you could get yourself killed.'

I'm getting used to this kind of sensationalism but something tells me this guy is no drama queen. He says he grew up in Tepito, which even I've heard of. Tepito is the roughest neighbourhood in Mexico City. He says there are a lot of guys in that district who've gotten involved in kidnap and worse. I ask him if he'd agree to show me around. But he laughs. 'Stick to the dancing,' he says. 'And stay clear of Tepito.'

The next morning my head is hurting from the tequilas nearly as much as my feet are from the dancing. I can't shake the feeling that I need to get into Tepito. There's nothing in my guidebook about it but there is a mention of something just outside it that spikes my interest. It's one of the city's little visited tourist attractions. I decide to kill two birds with one stone. I'll take another taxi ride and at the same time pay a visit to Santa Muerte herself.

My taxi driver is surprised when I give him the address. 'You sure you wanna go there?'

Yup. On the way, I tell him why I'm in town and he gives me the usual story. Don't go messing around in that world. These guys will kill you. People get shot every day in Mexico City. That kind of thing. I know his heart is in the right place and I am, I suppose, a little apprehensive about what I'm actually going to do if I get kidnapped but so far all the cab drivers I've met have been friendly as pussy cats. But then he says something new. He tells me that his taxi is sublet to another guy in the evenings. Pretty standard practice, he says. Many legit licensed cabs will work a shift during the day and then give over their cars to whoever in the nighttime. And this is when the problems start. Because who knows what that car gets used for when he's not around.

'Is it possible that this car has been used for a kidnap?' I ask him.

'Of course.'

He drops me on the outskirts of Tepito and I walk the rest of the way, following the directions on my map. When I arrive, I'm not disappointed by what I find.

I'm standing by the side of a quiet road in central Mexico City looking at a shrine. A shrine of a four-foot-high skeleton wearing a long black wig, white gown and hood. In her right hand she holds a globe, in her left she wields a scythe, which looks like it could take you off at your knees. Around her neck she wears a crucifix and all around her are more occult images of skeletons, death and donations. Pesos, flowers and jewellery thrown at her feet, presumably from visiting worshippers.

It's a pretty surreal sight. There's even a store next door selling candles and flowers. It's the kind of scene you'd see at a church. Because that is exactly what this looks like: a religious place of worship.

While I'm taking it all in, a heavily tattooed guy wearing a white vest and low-hanging jeans comes crawling up the street. Crawling. On his hands and knees. Right past me. Weeping with sorrow. When he reaches the Santa Muerte statue, he prostrates himself, crying the whole time, muttering prayers, begging for her intercession. He throws a pile of money at her feet and then kneels in silent prayer for another couple of minutes before he gets up, crosses himself and walks away.

I want to take a closer look but it feels somehow inappropriate. I'm not a religious man. The Catholics had a good go at me when I was young but I made it out in one piece and never looked back. But still, old habits die hard. I decide to compromise so I drop to my knees and make like a pilgrim. Feels weird but I figure it's probably the most subtle way to check it out without drawing attention to myself. Up close I count the money and I'm impressed how much she's collected. There's some pretty large bills there.

While I'm kneeling, another large-set guy comes and kneels next to me. I take a crafty sideways look at him, but he spots me and looks up. It feels a bit like when you catch another guy's eye at the urinal. You wish you hadn't. Especially when he says 'Hi'. But I decide to seize the opportunity. He's the first local I've met and I figure maybe I can ask him what he knows about the area.

His name is Haimé and he is a bona fide local of Tepito. He says he comes to the Santa Muerte shrine from time to time to ask her to look after his friends, who are in prison. 'Prison in Mexico City is tough.' I think it's safe to assume that he's talking from first-hand experience. I ask him if it would be safe for me to take a look around Tepito.

He shakes his head. 'If you go into Tepito alone, you will lose everything. At best, you lose everything you own, at worst, you lose your life too.' But then he throws me a bone. 'But if I take you, you'll be safe.'

I wonder if I've started to become too gung-ho about all this. Desensitised to danger. I think about the people at home who I love, my family, my new girlfriend (later my wife, the Nawlins fortune-tellers were half right!) and wonder whether they'd be cross that I'm putting myself in the firing line again for a story. What happened in Buenos Aires was truly terrifying and it plays on my mind quite often. What if those guys, full of coke, had just flipped? What if a gun had gone off in my face? These are the kind of questions I don't like to ask myself very often. I sit back and take a moment to feel, to really feel, what it is and one word comes directly to mind: exhilaration. This is exhilarating. So again, as I follow a complete stranger into one of the world's most notoriously dangerous districts, I feel exhilarated.

The streets of Tepito are a labyrinth of stalls and shops selling everything from electronic goods to children's toys. Haimé stops frequently to bumps fists with one tough guy after another. They all wear the regulation baggy jeans and vest, heavy tattoos, gold chains and signet rings. Pretty quickly I realise that Haimé knows everyone who's anyone. He's a character, a face. They double-take on me, the vulnerable Gringo, but nobody says anything because I'm with Haimé.

When we stop at a perfume stall, Haimé introduces me to his friend. They chat for a minute while I take a closer look at the goods on sale. There are all the latest brands from scents by Calvin Klein to Victoria Beckham. I note to Haimé that the prices are pretty competitive. He chuckles and translates for his friend. 'Go on, show him,' says Haimé with a smirk and his friend disappears for a couple of minutes then returns with a white plastic carrier bag full of stuff. He looks around to be sure nobody is watching and then turns to say, 'Come with me.'

I follow Haimé and his mate down a tight side alley that runs behind his stall. We come to a small clearing behind the buildings. After the dark enclosed market, it's the first time I've seen the sky for a while so I have to squint a little until my eyes adjust. Haimé's friend leads me over to a low wall, he puts down the bag and pulls out an amateur chemistry set; a plastic bottle full of liquid, a pipette, a screwdriver set and an empty CK One aftershave bottle. The fact that we're standing in the open in broad daylight doesn't seem to bother him as he gets to work.

'The shops sell us the empty bottles,' he says while he carefully pipettes the fluid from the plastic bottle into the Calvin Klein bottle. 'The bottle costs eight dollars, the scent four.' He works quickly fixing a seal and nozzle to the bottle to make it look like it's brand-new, straight from the factory, and with that he's done. 'I sell this for fifteen dollars each,' he says, holding it up for me to inspect. It looks like the real thing. I can't tell the difference. He moves up to three hundred of these a week, which means he nets around nine hundred dollars. Not bad for a stall in a neighbourhood like this.

While we're talking a shady-looking group of men appear from around the corner and begin to watch us. Haimé and his friend share a look which I pick up on as not good and then suddenly Haimé says it's time to go. Everyone moves quickly and I just follow. We go back to the market where Haimé says his goodbyes and then we leave the way we came in. I was hoping to investigate more and maybe make some contacts that could help me find someone attached to secuestro express but Haimé shakes his head. 'It's not safe for you here any more. It's better if you go.'

I follow Haimé back through the side streets towards the edge of Tepito. He seems like a genuinely good guy. I'm so grateful that he's taken the time to show me around his neighbourhood. It is starting to get dark as we reach the main road. I shake Haimé›s hand, thank him for the tour and jump in a cab. I'm still buzzing from the experience and too distracted to remember to check who the driver is or whether his ID matches that on the car. As we drive away, he seems curious as to what a Gringo was doing in Tepito. Suddenly I wonder what kind of cab picks up people from Tepito. We fall into an uneasy conversation and he begins to explain to me his story.

'I used to work in the textiles market in the far north of town,' he says. 'But I got into trouble there when I got into a fight with a guy who was extorting money from me. One day he comes in and points a gun at my wife's head. That night I went and killed the guy. I killed him with a .44 single shot to the head.'

I take a breath. I was looking for a kidnapper. But instead I've stumbled across a murderer.

'I sold everything to get out of jail. I spent everything I had on a good lawyer and he got me off.' He tells me that for $140,000 he was able to grease the wheels of Mexican justice and secure his release, despite his open admission that he had committed homicide. Now he daren't go back to the market for fear of reprisals from his victim's family. So instead he's found a new job. I guess the obvious next step for you careerwise as a murderer in Mexico City is to become a taxi driver.

I wonder if he's ever been involved in kidnappings.

He laughs at the idea. 'I'm a family man,' he says, almost insulted at the suggestion that he would be involved in something so unsavoury. 'But I do know people. I can ask if they will talk to you.'

I've arranged to meet an undercover officer in the Mexico City police force. He will speak to me on the condition of anonymity. He's taking the anonymity thing pretty seriously because he wears his baseball cap pulled down almost covering his eyes. The main thing to know about him is that he's risen quickly through the ranks, which he says is by being good at his job and not asking too many questions.

I'm interested in how a typical attack happens. He lays it out for me. Usually the victim is targeted near to an ATM machine. He says 90 per cent of the victims are women because they are 'easier to intimidate'. Usually, they are pulled into a car where the kidnappers will tie them. Hands behind the back to keep them from running. Then, he says, a gun is produced and pushed into the victim's face, encouraging them to reveal PIN numbers for all their accounts. After that, together they will visit the ATMs until all the cards are maxed out.

When the crime is done, the victim is released and instructed to get out and walk away from the vehicle without looking back. In less than half an hour it is over.

'In most cases of secuestro express, police officers or ex-police officers are involved,' he says. 'It's common for them to either do it while they are on leave from duties, or if they are on suspension for doing something wrong, or even if they have just retired.'

But why are so many cops getting involved in such a violent crime?

He says it's from financial necessity. 'You must understand it is hard to find a job in this country once you have been a policeman. No company will accept an ex-police officer, not even a private security company will have you.'

The reason is that most people associate the police with corruption. So it's a catch-22: the police must get involved in crime because everyone thinks the cops are involved in crime.

If I'm to believe him, then the problem is even more serious than I thought. Like an epidemic where the doctors are spreading the disease. Very hard to cure something like that. I'm curious if he knows people personally, maybe people who he has worked with, who might be directly involved in kidnapping.

'Yes, I know people,' he says, 'colleagues, policemen I have worked with have told me that they have been involved.'

And him? Has he ever kidnapped anyone?

'No,' he says after a long pause. 'But in reality, it is tempting sometimes.' He says that he thinks about growing old and he knows that a police pension won't be enough to sustain him. 'Wages for cops are low so many cops will do a second job and taxi driving is common,' he explains. 'So if you are driving a taxi and another cop pulls you over, you just show your badge and he'll let you go.'

That gives the perfect cover for doing secuestro express.

One of the problems here is that so many people in Mexico no longer have respect for the police, that it has created a resentment among even honest police officers. He says that there is no trust left on either side and so the police force is vulnerable to corruption. 'When people don't have respect for the police, the officers come to resent the society and the government.'

Before he leaves, I ask if he might be able to introduce me to anyone involved in the secuestro express.

He offers me a piece of advice. Even before he speaks, I know I've heard it before. 'If I were you, I would stay away from them, I would not have any kind of contact with them as they are very dangerous people. People that can hurt you, people who have damaged and injured too many in the past.'

Of course he's right. But on my hunt to track down the world's criminals, I am starting to realise that there is a definite pattern emerging. At every step, just when I feel I have met the person who can help me to make the all-important breakthrough, that very same person warns me to stop looking, pack up and go home. Having already met some pretty dangerous criminals, I know that's never going to happen, but it's difficult to convince someone that, just because you've done this kind of thing before, they don't need to worry about you. The cop in Buenos Aires isn't that different to the cop in Mexico City: they both see atrocious violent crimes committed in their city every day and they're right to warn me off. But I need to make him see that I'm not going to take no for an answer.

I explain to the policeman that I only want to talk. I can do it on any terms necessary. My intention is not to expose anyone or to act as an agent for the law but rather to hear and try to understand where they might be coming from. I list off some of the other places and crimes that I have investigated in the past few years and reassure him that I am still very much alive enough to tell the tale. All I need is an introduction and a phone number and I'll do the rest.

He says he'll think about it.

I hop into another taxi to head back to my hotel for the night. I'm running through everything I've seen in Mexico City so far: a shrine for worshipping death, a cab driver who openly admits to murder, and now kidnapping police officers. It's one crazy town. But I still want to hear the story from someone who is directly involved. As I look out of the window wondering whether my police contact may come through with the goods for me I start to realise that we're heading in almost the opposite direction to my hotel. I make to ask the driver why that is but he is making a call. Then I hear him tell the person on the other end of the phone, 'I am taking a Canadian. Yes, he's in the back now.'

Whoa!

Even though I'm not Canadian, he's clearly talking about me. Why would he be having that conversation? Why are we going the wrong way? I find myself shouting 'Stop!'

He looks at me baffled for a moment and then pulls over. 'Are you okay?'

'I'm going to get out here,' I say and throw him one hundred pesos. 'Keep the change.' I jump out.

The taxi drives off and I can feel the panic subside a little. Am I being paranoid? Maybe this was just a simple 'long way round' scam that I've seen a hundred times before all over the world. The driver recognises you're a tourist and takes you via the most circuitous route just to make a few extra dollars on the fare. It could have been as innocent as that but Mexico has clearly got me rattled. All I could see was impending kidnap. But would he have let me out if he was a kidnapper? And if he was a kidnapper, isn't that exactly what I've been looking for?

I suddenly feel silly. Either I've imagined the whole thing and given myself a long walk home. Or I've found what I was looking for and run away scared. Neither option leaves me feeling very good about myself.

I decide a walk is the best thing for me and set off on foot to my hotel.

The next morning, I wake with a new resolve. I am going to find a kidnapper in Mexico if it's the last thing I do. This is without doubt the riskiest interview I've attempted. But I'm going to head into the lion's den one more time. I call the cop and tell him that I've thought about everything he said last night but I'm serious and either he helps me find someone involved in secuestro express or I'm going to keep getting in cabs until I get kidnapped myself.

He calls me back later that day. Someone will call me. I should do exactly what they say. He can't guarantee anything and he wants to make it very clear that he cannot be held responsible if anything should go wrong. He repeats his advice. Don't do this.

True to his word I get a call later in the afternoon from someone who says they got my number from the cop. It's not a kidnapper but a private security company. They want to meet up so we arrange to rendezvous in a bar near my hotel.

That evening I'm sitting at the bar waiting for my meeting and order a rum and lime while I think through my options. I'm not particularly keen to follow through on my threat to just keep getting in cabs until I get kidnapped for real. So this is my best bet. I need to trust that the cop knows what he's doing.

Two guys the size of gorillas, dressed in black and making no effort to conceal their weapons, come into the bar. I can tell instantly they are the guys I'm here to meet. They grab a couple of beers and we find a quiet corner to talk. The bigger one explains to me that they are retired police officers who have moved into the security business. They do mostly private protection work for high-worth individuals in Mexico City. Bodyguards. The deal they have for me is that I will employ them to protect me while I conduct an interview with a prolific kidnapper who they will arrange for me to meet. They say the guy is extremely dangerous but that they are confident that an interview can be arranged that is secure as long as I am under their protection.

I weigh up my options. From experience, I suspect that these guys are as bent as, well as bent as a Mexican policeman. But I'm reassured that everyone is being open about money and they're making no pretence that this is anything other than a transaction. Are they themselves involved in kidnapping? It's hard to tell. Back at my hotel, I do a background check on them online and their security business at least seems legitimate.

I decide to go for it as long as I can get some kind of insurance. I want to be doubly protected. I put in a call to London to an insurance broker I've used before. I want to find out how far my insurance will cover me, mainly that if something were to go wrong and I got myself kidnapped for real, that there was enough money to pay for a decent search party. For journalists working in the field there are special insurance policies to cover exactly this kind of situation. The broker doesn't sound fazed. He says there's a policy to cover this, a Kidnap and Ransom policy, but it would cost a pretty penny. It's the same insurance policy often used by corporate contractors operating in war zones and high-profile individuals like celebrities and politicians when they're in places like Mexico.

The broker says I can get cover but the premium is so expensive that it's better to pay it by the minute. So I need to initiate the policy with a call to the UK the second I am alone with the kidnapper. Then I call again the second I am safely away from the potential kidnap situation to stop the clock. In the event that something goes wrong, the insurer will immediately swing into action, deploying specialists to assist in my release. This includes specialist negotiators, delivery of any ransom demanded, evacuation and any subsequent psychiatric care. One thing they insist on is that I never disclose that I have kidnap insurance to anyone. In high-risk areas, telling the wrong person that you are covered to pay a million-dollar ransom is tantamount to wearing a T-shirt that says 'KIDNAP ME!'

Of course it doesn't always work out. Last month the niece of the Spanish international footballer, Angel María Villar, was kidnapped. María Villar Glaz was in town working for IBM when she evidently got into the wrong taxi. She seemingly became a typical victim of secuestro express because from her bank records police know that she was taken to a few ATMs and forced to withdraw cash. But then something changed.

Maybe the kidnappers worked out who she was because, rather than releasing her, they contacted her family and demanded a ransom of 2 million pesos (US$100,000). María's husband engaged local negotiators to help secure her release and on their advice he countered with a lower offer. María's body was found, dumped in a sewer, two days later. She had been asphyxiated with a plastic bag.

Her death came as a big shock to family, friends and government officials, all of whom expected the thirty-nine-year-old to be released. But criminals aren't always predictable.

Gorilla number one and gorilla number two pick me up the next evening and together we drive to a quiet side street around five blocks away. Their car is equipped with a small arsenal. Both of them are sporting Glock hand-guns in holsters and gorilla two has an automatic rifle in the footwell between his legs. We pull up directly behind a small hatchback car parked along the street. The interview will be conducted inside the car. They say that this is the safest option. Everyone can see what everyone else is doing and only they have the keys to the car.

They escort me to the parked car and I take a seat in the back. My heart is banging like a drum inside my chest. I make the call to the insurance company to initiate the search-and-rescue policy. And I wait.

A minute later, a large heavyset man with a baseball cap pulled down low over his eyes approaches the car and slides into the back seat next to me. We shake hands. 'Mucho Gusto.' He sizes me up. I can smell the adrenalin coming off him too. Why do these guys do it? Why take the risk to turn up and get asked questions about the serious criminal activity that you're engaged in? Maybe he's on a cut of the fee I'm paying the security guys. But would that be sufficient to motivate taking such a risk?

No, I don't think so. I think that, again, this a guy who just wants to talk.

I wonder if he's from Mexico City. He is. I wonder what growing up here was like, did he encounter crime? Gangs?

'Yes,' he says. 'When you grow up here, you meet the people who are in charge of trading guns, drugs, and all those things.'

And was he involved in gangs?

'No. I had regular jobs, construction, taxi driver and then I became a Federal District police officer.' He pauses and looks out of the window for a moment. 'But things went wrong and I ended up in jail.' What happened? He shakes his head. He doesn't want to say. 'That's where I met people involved with secuestro express.'

Just like the cop said, this is a retired police officer who has moved into the kidnap business. I press him a little on what exactly he went to jail for. He'll only say that he took the rap for something several of his colleagues were involved in. Corruption of some form. But when he got out, the new contacts he'd made on the inside invited him to get involved in the 'business'.

He says that the group has been working together now for a few years. 'For this, a group of three or four people is needed. An express kidnapping is made in the least possible amount of time. We locate the person, could be going out from a shopping mall, from a bank, from their house. Many times these are people we have already identified beforehand.'

I hadn't realised so much planning goes into it. I had always heard it was more speculative than that.

'We use weapons,' he says. 'I mean, in order to intimidate the person you need to scare them, so they do what you are asking them to do. And if we manage to get information beforehand about their family – their children, the wife – then using that we can intimidate them. Tell them that if they don't cooperate with us, their family will see the consequences.'

He reckons that he has personally been involved in over seventy kidnappings. Most of them, he says, were women, backing up my earlier information that they are more easily intimidated. In some cases, his gang has got really lucky: 'The maximum we make is 150,000 pesos (US$1,500), but it's fast, it's a matter of two or three hours, tops. But in some cases it can last up to a day or two. If they give the amount that we asked for it's okay and we let them free. Many times the intimidated person is scared and doesn't need to be hurt or tortured. They'll give up on their own.'

His advice is that this is the best course of action for anyone who is kidnapped. Do exactly as you're told and you won't get hurt.

Then I notice it, hanging around his neck. A small figurine depicting Santa Muerte herself. I point it out to him. 'Yes, that's my Santa Muerte.' He touches it as he gets out of the car. 'She's the one who takes care of us. I wear it for protection.' It was his insurance policy. Which reminds me, I have to make a phone call.

Again, I've found a darkness in Latin America. Like many parts of the region crime here seems to be fuelled by an intoxicating mix of guns and hard drugs. But what is unique to Mexico is the looming presence of religion. Religion has often been used in times of war to justify the evil acts of men. Here on the streets of Mexico City, things are not so different. Evil men can do evil things with impunity because they have the saints on their side.

CHAPTER SEVEN

TARIQ FROM HEBRON

'You want to see a mummy?'

WHEN I WAS a kid, the *Antiques Roadshow* was on TV right before *The A-Team* so I'd usually catch the last ten minutes. The bit I enjoyed was right after the experts revealed that the old vase from granny's attic was worth enough money to buy a holiday in the Bahamas. Everyone would nod sagely, trying to keep a straight face while earnestly discussing the vase's artistic merit, but I knew that inside they were already packing their suitcases.

I admire those who have dedicated themselves to becoming knowledgeable about the past. Our culture, our heritage, the fabric of who we are as a society, is wrapped up in the beautiful things our forebears have created. And there's no shortage of people who'll pay a pretty penny to have a piece of it hanging on their wall.

You can add a whole extra dimension when you factor in religion. Religion is big business. Rome, Mecca and Jerusalem between them attract over 20 million visitors annually. For many pilgrims, this is a once-in-a-lifetime trip – a mix of vacation and religious duty. People save for their whole lives to visit these places and part of the budget includes a line for souvenirs.

Jerusalem, in particular, has capitalised on being one of the oldest cities in the world. It has become an epicentre for the trade in ancient antiquities between East and West. From the souks of the Arab Quarter to the auction rooms of West Jerusalem, there's a roaring trade going on in Jerusalem for artefacts from the past.

But what about someone like me? Someone who knows nothing about what is genuinely an antique or not? Or worse still, someone who knows as little as me and also has a burning religious zeal to acquire a valuable memento of their once-in-a-lifetime religious pilgrimage? This person could suddenly appear to be quite vulnerable.

That's exactly why I've come to Jerusalem.

Or at least it would be if I could make it out of the airport.

I've been stopped. Pulled over. Excuse me, sir, would you mind following me. My passport taken and led to a 'quiet room' where I'm told to take a seat. No number of 'Is there a problem, officer's seems to elicit a response. Someone will call you. No we don't have any water.

In the quiet room with me is a young family. Father, mother and one child. From the way they are dressed, I can tell they are Muslim. The child is bored and irritable and the mother is desperately trying to find things in her handbag with which to distract him.

After around forty minutes, a flat-footed spook comes into the room and calls my name. I follow him to a brightly lit, cramped office where he tells me to take a seat across the desk from him. The air-con machine splutters like a ruptured lung in the corner. The room has a tatty-looking map of Israel on the wall and an old PC on the desk but otherwise it's as bare as stone. He ignores me for a couple of minutes while he thumbs through my passport. He sighs heavily. I get the whiff of stale instant coffee off his breath.

Mr Woodman? he asks. That's me. Is there a problem? What is the purpose of your visit to Jerusalem? I'm here doing a story on antiques. He pauses at the various stamps in the back of my passport. He seems particularly interested in the ones with Arabic script. Why were you in Sudan? A story about camels. Camels? Yes. I went there to buy some. He looks at me as though I am joking but I'm not.

And Afghanistan? he asks. Poppies I reply. He stares at me. You know, the ones you make heroin from. I'm having fun now. I am aware that this guy can make my life very difficult but I haven't done anything wrong. Mr Woodman, he says sternly. Yes? I say all innocently. Why are you interested in heroin? I come clean and explain that I write and make programmes about a wide range of topics all over the world. So I was in Sudan for camels, Afghanistan for poppies and now Jerusalem for antiques. What is the problem?

The problem of course is that Israel has many enemies and when you have many enemies you become paranoid that everyone is a potential enemy. My passport indicates that I have travelled extensively in the Muslim world. I have stamps from Arabic North African countries like Morocco, Egypt and Sudan as well as Middle Eastern states like Lebanon and a few of the 'Stans', including Afghanistan. So I am being held in this room because, as far as the state of Israel is concerned, I might be an enemy. Which of course is ridiculous. If I was a serious enemy then the first thing I would do would be to get a new passport.

Do you have any identification?

I look at my passport in his hand. You're holding it. That is my identification. That is the most official document I have and it is widely regarded in the free world as proof of who I am. Is that not the case here too? Do you have any reason to suspect that I am not who I say I am? He bristles when I say 'free'.

Israel has become so paranoid about its enemies that it has built a wall around itself to keep them out. Palestine, the land that Israel still occupies, has literally been fenced off so that its people are no longer free to move around their own country.

I'm afraid I'm going to need to see some other credentials, he says.

This is becoming uncomfortable. I ask him whether I've been screened. He won't say. I ask him why he has singled me out, if I have been flagged on some sort of Mossad security system. He won't say. I ask him if he has Google on his computer. He says, 'What?' Google. I repeat. Does the Israeli security budget extend as far as having use of the Internet? Of course it does, he spits back at me. Well, why don't you try typing 'Conor Woodman' into Google and see what you get then, I say. According to B'Taselem, a non-profit human rights organisation, Mossad, the Israeli secret service, has been responsible for over 500 'targeted killings' on Palestinian citizens since 2002. So when someone on the other side of the wall is determined to be bad for business, Mossad takes them out or, worse still, they fly over and take out their entire block. This was their policy in 2009 when Israel launched airstrikes on Palestinian civilians, which the UN say killed 1,400 people including over 300 children. And again was their policy in 2014 when their firebombs murdered another 2,200 Palestinians, including 555 children.

The fear of retribution clearly runs deep. As I sit in this grubby little room, it occurs to me that, despite a career that has called for me to fly regularly around the world, often to troubled, war-torn places, I am being interrogated for the first time. Even though I have done nothing wrong, the man sitting opposite me would rather work on the basis that I have. I am aware that this is a place twisted by paranoia and fear. Such a dysfunctional environment creates exactly the right conditions for those who would profit from getting up to no good. As an innocent man I am indignant, but as a man looking for criminals, I am perversely optimistic.

The Israeli security man types my name into the Internet search engine. I watch his face change as he scrolls down the screen. He hands back the passport and tells me I am free to go. I wonder about what I would have done had I not had a job in the media that gave me the luxury of an Internet profile. I wonder about how long the family in the waiting room might have to remain while they try to reassure him of their 'credentials'. But mostly I wonder how this country got itself into such a mess.

Once safely into the city, I decide to do some reconnaissance. I take a walk to get a measure of the place as it's many years since I was here last.

One thing that hasn't changed is the cultural diversity on show. People in Jerusalem are fiercely tribal and one of the favourite ways to demonstrate that is by what they wear on top of their heads. A middle-aged Jewish man lost in conversation on his phone rushes past me wearing the large woolly shtreimel favoured by many Hassidic

Jews. He nearly trips over a child's buggy. The mother, a young Ultra-Orthodox Jewish woman, hair tied back with a heavy black tichel, tuts quietly to herself. An old Arabic man smiles as he hobbles past with his cane, his long white kufiya draped halfway down his back. Everywhere I see scenes like this played out in yammakahs and snoods, taqiyas, hijabs and sudras. You ain't nobody in Jerusalem if you ain't got a hat.

Most of the tourist action occurs within the ancient walls of the old city. Walk along the tight and narrow cobbled streets of this part of town and you'll spot that the shops owners are predominantly Arab, hence why it's commonly known as the Arab Quarter. Were it not for the huge Star of David flag draped provocatively from the walls of a building owned by Ariel Sharon, you'd think you were in an Arab country.

The streets of the Arab Quarter are cut from smooth white stone that glares back at you so that sunglasses are essential. Along the streets, shallow awnings shelter the fruit and spices on sale from small carts, while hole-in-the-wall shops offer electronics and rugs. The shopkeepers loudly call out deals to catch the passing trade. The passageways often narrow so much that a surge of passing tourists can make you feel terribly claustrophobic.

And there are many tourists in this part of town. Because this is also the area through which Jesus Christ was led to his crucifixion.

Many of the shops along Jesus' actual route, the Via Dolorosa, are named after the particular station of the cross that depicts his walk. You can buy fruit where he fell for the second time, you can buy sandals at the spot where Shimon of Aramaia mopped his brow and you can buy antiquities at any number of shops in between. It is in these shops that I have decided to begin my investigation.

The first shop I pick is run by a shopkeeper in his mid-thirties, a Jewish man dressed in the regulation white shirt and black waistcoat that guys in this part of town all seem to wear. I'm surprised because I'd expected all the shops to be Arab-owned. But he's thoroughly charming and seemingly very knowledgeable about the various things he says I could afford on my budget. He has coins, rings and various pieces of pottery that he says all stem from the ancient past. He tells me that he and his father, a gentleman in his mid-sixties sitting in the corner, have over sixty years in the antiques business between them. After some deliberation and a bit of hard sell from the old guy, I decide to buy a fragment of pottery, which he says was made sometime around the time of Jesus. It's a modest purchase, clay, around two inches square with some writing the father tells me is ancient Hebrew. 'It was found in Masada,' he says. It's all neatly boxed up for me and comes with a certificate of authenticity signed by the owner himself. As he signs the document, he assures me this will guarantee its resale value if ever I choose to cash in on my 'good investment'.

I'm keen to find out just how good an investment I've made so I have enlisted the help of world-renowned art historian Shimon Gibson, Professor of Archaeology at the University of North Carolina. Despite his name, Shimon is a Brit. He turns up looking every inch the part; multi-pocket khaki green vest, khaki trousers, boots and hat. Think Indiana Jones in *The Temple of Doom*.

Shimon has written books on Middle Eastern art and he specialises in relics and artefacts found in what is now Israel and Palestine. Although he's born in the UK, he's made the Middle East his life's work. Now he says that the market is flooded with fakes, some of which are very good. Good enough to fool even the experts. 'Even the Israeli museum here in Jerusalem has been fooled by fakes,' he says. The Israel museum bought a pomegranate jug back in 1988 for $550,000, paid into a numbered Swiss bank account. For more than twenty years, it was hailed as the only surviving physical evidence of the First Temple. Until it turned out to be a fake.

We grab a coffee at the cafe round the corner and I carefully unwrap my purchase to show Shimon. What does he reckon? Good value for a hundred pounds?

Shimon carefully inspects the piece. He runs his finger along the cracks in the pottery that have been formed by thousands of years of ageing and he tilts it slightly to read the fragments of Hebrew etched onto its side. I didn't know you spoke Hebrew, I say. 'Yes, I do. But this isn't Hebrew. It's French.'

Now I'm pretty sure that nobody around Palestine was speaking French two thousand years ago. But then this piece of clay wasn't around two thousand years ago either.

'What you have here,' says Shimon in his best *Antiques Roadshow* voice, 'Is a one hundred per cent genuine, broken fragment of a French roof tile, which if we look closer at the inscription ...' He holds it up to the light so that I can get a good look. '... could originally have said "Fabriqué à Marseille".' It didn't happen like this on *Antiques Roadshow*. 'Look up there,' he says, pointing towards the roof opposite. As I follow his arm, I realise that all the roofs in this part of town are covered in similar tiles to the one he's holding. It seems I've been had.

Time to go back to the shop.

Father and son are a little surprised to see me again so soon. I guess shopkeepers all over the world dread the returning customer. But I want these guys to feel relaxed so I flash them my breeziest smile to reassure them all is well. I'm not here for a confrontation. I just want information. If even the museums, with all their experts on the payroll, can be fooled by a good fake, this could all be an innocent mistake.

At the counter they watch as I carefully unwrap the clay 'artefact' with its 'certificate of authenticity'. Together they take a very close look at it. I'm desperately trying to read them. Are they going to feign innocence? To my surprise they take the opposite strategy and, hard as you like, they go instead into full confrontation mode.

'No, no, no.' They both start repeating over and over.

The father holds the piece up to me like an exhibit at a trial. 'This is genuine.'

I point out all the things Shimon showed me, including the French inscription. But they stick to their guns, they feign insult, they get very dramatic indeed. Then the son produces a Bible. A Bible. The Jewish man produces the Christian book, lays his right hand on it and vows, 'I swear that I did not know this was a piece of tile.'

They totally knew it was a fake.

We dance around for another fifteen minutes. I stand my ground as they try one explanation after another. None of which are particularly convincing. Eventually they concede that 'maybe' the piece isn't genuine. But, they say, if that is the case then it is they who are the victims because they bought the piece from someone else who told them it was genuine. Reluctantly they offer me a full refund but they maintain it's all just an innocent mistake.

What I do for a living is counter-intuitive to most people. This is a prime example. I am in a shop where I have been deceived, deliberately or not, into buying a fake. And because of this, I am delighted. I am thrilled. This is exactly what I wanted to happen. Because this is the kind of break that I was looking for. But this feeling is hard to convey to a defensive shopkeeper who himself feels he is being accused of wrong-doing. What I have to do is to make him feel at ease, when his instinct is to try to make me feel at ease. It confuses a lot of people.

I tell the men that I am not seeking a refund. I'm perfectly happy to keep the piece. I even accept their story and sympathise that they too have been fooled by some unscrupulous person. I don't believe that for a second, because not so long ago they told me they had sixty years of experience between them. But I play along. What I really want to know, I explain, is where this broken roof tile came from. I want to learn more about how fakes like this reach the market. I don't want a refund; I want information.

This is when the mood in the shop takes a sudden turn. The son raises both of his hands as though I am pointing a gun at his head and turns away from me. The father stops dead still and looks nervously towards the door. It's like a ghost came through the walls. 'Why are you asking these things?' says Dad. 'These are not things that concern you.' He tries to grab the roof tile from my hand but I pull it away just in time. 'I give you a refund and then you go.'

I've struck a nerve. I explain myself again. I don't want money. I want to know where the fakes come from. I can feel the tension go up another notch.

'I cannot speak about these things.' He's angry now. 'You want me to get killed?'

Killed? That seems a little strong. Why would anyone want to kill him?

'The people who make this,' he says, pointing again at the tile. 'If they hear that I talk about this, then in twenty-four hours, I might be dead. Even you. You should take care. Why should you go to the root of these dirty things?' And with that he raises his hands to indicate the conversation is over. He offers me a refund again but when I refuse again, he asks me to leave.

I'm clearly on the right path, I just need to try to find someone who will talk. Shimon agrees to accompany me on a more extensive shopping trip, this time through the Arab shops in the Arab Quarter. We walk along the Via Dolorosa casing some of the shops and working out which ones might be the best to target.

Shimon suggests we use a code. If I pick out a piece that he thinks is genuine, then he'll say, 'that's good'. If I pick out a piece and he thinks it's a fake then he'll say 'that's very good'. If it's a total sham rip-off then he'll say it's 'very very good'. This way the shop owners won't realise what we're up to and we can get them to show us a good range of their wares before they get suspicious.

We start with a shop around the third station of the cross. Next to the plaque depicting the spot where Christ fell for the first time is an Arab-owned antiques store clearly aimed at tourists making pilgrimage. There are large glass display cases filled with ancient relics for you to take home at a tidy price. Pots and bowls, plates and coins, tools and tiles, there's a huge variety of souvenirs from which to choose. The shop owner, a heavyset man with an enormous moustache, approaches and asks if we need help. I ask him about an old stone statuette in one of the glass cases that Shimon has just described as 'unbelievably good'.

He unlocks the door and takes it out for me to have a closer look at. 'That is Jesus,' he says.

So how old is it?

'It's two thousand years old.'

Interesting. A statue of Jesus, carved in his own lifetime. That would be the only existing statue of its kind. In the world. Ever. How much?

'I give you this for three hundred dollars.'

Bargain. I buy it for three hundred dollars.

At the next shop, the works in the cabinets look a bit more upmarket. It's a labyrinth of rooms full of beautiful-looking artefacts and jewellery and Shimon is impressed with some of the work. 'This is good,' he says looking at an old clay pot. He nods appreciatively. Obviously genuine. I'm looking at it next to everything else and again feel so helpless. I, like most people, have no clue as to what might be real or not. The guys from the *Antiques Roadshow* could film a whole series here.

Shimon calls me over to have a look at a particular piece. 'This is very very good,' he says.

Code word acknowledged, I ask the shopkeeper if I can take a look.

'Good choice, sir,' he says. 'This is a Roman cup dating back over two thousand years.'

Shimon is trying hard to contain his smirk as I take a closer look at the small green glass tumbler. It looks pretty genuine to me but I'll defer to Shimon's expertise.

'It's really very very excellent.' He's getting a little carried away.

'How much?' I ask and then we have a little haggle. In the interest of maintaining my cover, I have decided that I must haggle. I also just enjoy haggling. I get him down to a hundred dollars for the cup and he wraps it up for me.

Outside Shimon and I find a quiet corner to inspect the two pieces we've bought. 'The Jesus sculpture is just ridiculous,' says Shimon. 'We don't have even drawings of Jesus from before the late second century.'

What about the Roman cup? It seems so genuine.

'It's a good copy,' he says. 'That's why I was so drawn to it. Whoever made this knows what they're doing.'

But Shimon shows me why it's not the real deal. The

patina, the weathered layer on the surface of the glass, he says has been fabricated rather than naturally caused by time. 'This is how they make it look older than it really is. But this was made in a workshop somewhere not far from here and certainly not during the Roman Empire.'

I'm so grateful to Shimon for all his help. He's given me the ammunition I need to push my investigation to the next stage. So, armed with all the benefits of his encyclopaedic knowledge, I return first to the Arab shop where we bought what I am now calling the 'Jesus Stone', the statue of the Christ allegedly carved two thousand years ago.

I recognise the owner right away when he makes his approach but I don't feel any recognition from him so I have to remind him that I was in the shop minutes earlier. His face changes and he suddenly looks rather suspicious of me. His eyes dart back and forth between me and the item I'm carrying. I love this bit of the process of confronting scam artists. I'm tingling with the buzz of it. I wonder if this guy will crack and open up to me. The key is to remain non-confrontational at all times. Just like the Jewish guys who sold me the roof tile, the key is to make sure he doesn't feel in any way threatened.

I remind him that I bought this statue of Jesus earlier in the day and then I recall some of the details of what he told me. I remind him about how he said that the statue was two thousand years old but I say that if that were true, then it would be the only known statue in the existence of Jesus made in his own lifetime. He starts to look uncomfortable so I pull back.

'Look,' I say. 'I know that this isn't a two-thousand-year-old statue of Jesus. That's not why I'm here. I'm not here to cause any trouble.'

He calls into the next room in Arabic and another man, who looks like a relative, comes in. Then he turns to me. 'You are lying.' His voice is a little raised.

I try to reassure him again that there's no problem, I only want to find out more about where the statue came from. But his mood has darkened considerably. He takes me by the arm and starts pushing me towards the door. 'You are a liar!' he shouts at me. He shouts it louder and louder. 'Liar. Liar.' He keeps pushing me. I want only to talk with him but I can't even begin the conversation because he's pushing me and shouting. I feel more than a little threatened.

'Sir,' I appeal to him. 'I bought this statue from you in good faith. I am not a liar.'

He gives me another shove towards the stairs. 'I never sold you anything. You are stupid.' Okay, so it looks like this guy isn't for turning. I change approach. 'How am I stupid?' I ask.

'You are shit!' he shouts. 'Get out. Get out. I will not sell you anything. You are shit. You are shit!'

My heart is racing because there's a risk this could turn nasty. His relatives are now gathered around him and I'm halfway back down the stairs to the street. He pursues me, screaming at me over and over, 'Get out. Get out. You are shit!' People on the street are stopping to look and see what is happening but he is undeterred, screaming at me until eventually I have no option but to leave.

I guess I will have to chalk this one down as a 'doesn't want to cooperate'.

A little rattled, I try to compose myself. This wasn't the plan. I get nothing from the confrontation other than a racing pulse and a sense of deflation. I didn't come to Jerusalem to get into fights with shopkeepers and I've now blown one of my two leads. I couldn't care less about the money, but I do care about the missed opportunity to find out more about its provenance. I have to be more careful.

I gather myself and walk up the Via Dolorosa past the fourth station, where Christ met his mother. I wish mine was here right now, she knows better than anyone I know how to return goods to a shop! But I am alone on this quest. I duck back into the shop where I bought the Roman cup and give the shopkeeper my biggest warmest smile. I shake his hand earnestly and ask him how he is and bow my head to play low status to him. I apologise for troubling him again. Confident that he is in no way threatened by me, I apologise again and ask him if he might give me some advice.

'Of course, my friend,' he says, offering me a seat at his desk.

I sit and explain to him why I have returned. I tell him again how sorry I am and that I come to ask only for his opinion and not to make any complaint. I tell him that I love my Roman cup but that my friend, an eminent scholar of the period, suggested that it might be a fake. I repeat that I am not seeking to return the item but only to ask him in his professional opinion what he thinks of my friend's assessment. I even tell him the story about the Israel museum being fooled into buying fakes. He eyes me with a degree of suspicion but he seems calm. He asks if he can look again at the cup. So I unwrap the cup and hand it to him.

The shopkeeper's name is Ali and I instantly get the feeling that he does not believe the cup is a fake. 'I'm not an expert,' he says, looking closely at it. 'And I think it is not a fake but if you think it is then you must have your money back.'

He starts to take money out of his pocket before I stop him and explain my story. I just want info. I want help to find people who know more about the process of making fakes. Ali seems pretty relaxed about my request. 'Yes, there are people I know who do this,' he says. 'But I'll have to ask them if they will meet with you.'

This is brilliant. A break. And importantly a contact.

I'm curious as to why Ali seems open to talk about it when others have been so defensive, paranoid even. He says that the people he knows are not directly connected to merchants in the city. He says that his shop never buys fakes and he maintains that the Roman cup is genuine, despite what Shimon says. But nonetheless, whatever happens, he says the meeting cannot happen anywhere near his shop. 'Better that it happens even outside of Jerusalem,' he says.

I'm so grateful. I really like Ali. I believe him when he says that he doesn't think the cup is a fake. I believe him when he says that he will help me to meet the right people. I wonder, as I often do, why a stranger would help another stranger to find out about these 'dirty things', as the Jewish shopkeeper called them. I'm not sure what the answer is. Sometimes people surprise you. Maybe Ali wants to prove to me that he is an honest man. Maybe this is his way of showing me that the people involved in manufacturing fakes are not the same as him. Either way, he's going to help me. And for that I am so grateful.

Later that evening I try to get hold of Ali on his mobile but it is switched off. The next day I try again but again it is off. I decide I will have to return to the shop to speak directly with him. Perhaps he has gotten cold feet.

I take a cab back towards the Arab Quarter. My driver is a local Arab called Waled and his cab is a rather finely appointed Mercedes with excellent air-conditioning, a welcome relief in the thirty-degree heat. Waled says he owns several taxis as well as a tour guide service to the city. He's a genuine entrepreneur and keen to sell me his services. I tell him why I'm heading to the Arab Quarter. I tell him about the fake artefacts that I've bought and how Ali has offered to help me. When we reach the gate to the old city, I take his card and promise to call again when I'm ready to leave.

I walk back along the Via Dolorosa and eventually reach Ali's shop. He is with a customer when I arrive but he clocks me out of the corner of his eye and points me to his desk. I can't read the situation. Does he look a little shifty today? It's hard to tell. His customer doesn't buy anything and leaves. Ali comes over to join me. He doesn't hang around. 'I called my contacts but they said they don't want to talk with you,' he says. 'I think they are scared to talk.'

He looks sorry but despite my best attempts to persuade him to try again or to put me in contact directly, I begin to realise that this is as much as I'm going to get. I've reached a dead end.

Back outside, a group of tourists pass by. The middle-aged man at the head of the group is carrying a crucifix and the group are reciting a rosary in German. They head up the hill towards the Church of the Holy Sepulchre and I call Waled, the taxi driver, for a lift back to my hotel. Deflated, I trudge back down the hill.

Waled arrives at the gate in his Merc. He's smiling and waving as he pulls up. I hop in and he turns round to greet me. 'Good news,' he says. 'I have found a man who makes fake artefacts. I can take you to meet him tomorrow.'

I sit in stunned silence. I trudged up and down that hot dusty road. I went undercover, got screamed at, thrown out of shops, warned about bad men who might hurt me and all along all I really needed to do was ask a taxi driver where to find what I was looking for!

'Just one thing,' says Waled. 'The man cannot come across the wall. You will have to go to the occupied territories to meet him.'

The next morning Waled collects me in the Merc and we drive east out of the city towards the West Bank. After half an hour we reach 'the wall', a huge security fence built by the Israeli government between 2000 and 2003 to limit movement between West Jerusalem and the occupied Palestinian Territories to the north and east. The wall takes the form of several security fences as high as a two-storey house and topped with rolls and rolls of razor wire. There are checkpoints all along it at which heavily armed Israeli soldiers perform routine checks on vehicles passing through. It is one of the most depressing things I have ever seen.

Waled and I sit in silence as we pass through the checkpoints and come out on the other side. In Palestine.

A few miles further on we stop on the side of the dusty main road to Ramallah and wait until an unremarkable white transit van pulls up along the hard shoulder next to us. I climb up inside next to an Arab man who we can call Tariq. Tariq is nervous. He's asked to meet here because as a Palestinian he can't move freely across the wall, and in his home town in Palestine where he has an antiques shop, people wouldn't be very agreeable to him answering questions from a journalist.

I start by telling Tariq my story so far. I tell him that I've been undercover in the shops and market stalls in Jerusalem looking for fake artefacts. I tell him that with the help of an academic I have already established that the market for artefacts is flooded with fakes. He nods and shrugs as I speak; evidently this is not news to him.

So I tell him what I'm interested in now is going back a little bit further in the chain to find a little more information about some of the fakes and in particular how they find their way into Jerusalem and end up in the shops where the tourists come and buy them.

I'm surprised when Tariq tells me that first I must understand that he is passionate about antiques. He says he is in his last semester now of a master's degree in antiquities. Despite nearly thirty years in the business of selling the stuff, he decided a couple of years ago to study hard so he could understand more about what was passing through his hands. He says the course has totally opened his eyes to the horror of the business and that fakes are only the tip of the iceberg.

Tariq says there's been a long-standing tradition of counterfeiting antiques in the West Bank. Old coins are the easiest end of the business to make money on. 'They can counterfeit old coins easy,' he says. Like a magician, he produces a bag of ancient shekels from his pocket and spills them out on the seat between us. 'Tourists will buy these for up to twenty dollars apiece, but the guy making them sells them for a shekel or two (about fifty to ninety US cents).' He's scornful of this practice. 'There's no big money here,' he says, despite the fact that he has his own bag of counterfeit old coins in his pocket. 'You make a few dollars but this kind of thing it only ruins the antique business.'

It's touching that Tariq seems to care about the reputation of the trade at the same time as being prepared to turn a quick buck from corrupting it. It's a sort of can't beat them, join them attitude. I wonder if he's educating himself out of self-protection as much as self-improvement. Knowledge is definitely power in this business.

'I want to tell you more,' says Tariq. 'I want to tell you but not harm myself.'

I reassure Tariq that I will change his name. I'm surprised he's so fearful when after all we're only talking about pennies and dollars, this is hardly mafia territory.

'No not that, the antique authorities.' He shakes his head. 'I have cases from previous dealings.'

I want Tariq to tell me what he thinks of my fakes. I

show him the glass cup I bought in the Arab Quarter. 'This is old. I think this is old, but not from here. This is coming from Iraq.' What? I tell him that's not what Shimon said. I tell him a renowned professor confirmed that this cup was a fake most likely made in a workshop somewhere here in Palestine. Tariq shakes his head. 'Listen,' he says. 'I have fakes in my shop. I know fakes. The Professor is making a mistake.' I find this unlikely. 'Even the Israeli museum can make a mistake and buy a fake,' says Tariq. 'They bought two pieces of glass from Syria and Lebanon.' He's referring to a recent now famous case of the Israeli museum being tricked into buying counterfeits. Tariq's point is that if it can happen to one of the world's greatest museums then it can happen to anyone.

He shows me the cup. 'Look carefully,' he says. 'This glass is not from here. It is from Iraq.' He runs his finger along the patina pointing out where the dirt is ingrained deep into the glass. 'You cannot fake this. This is Byzantine, Roman, but not from here, from Iraq. Many pieces like this are coming here now from Iraq and Egypt and Syria.'

Fake or real, I ask?

'Real. Real. Real,' he says like I've finally caught up with him. 'I can tell you things that would make your head spin.'

I'm starting to get the feeling that I'm uncovering a different story to the one I came looking for. My suspicion was that Tariq was my way into a counterfeiting and smuggling network that linked forgery workshops on the Palestinian side of the wall to the tourist-rich Israeli side. But from what Tariq is saying, the business has evolved.

'I can show you a bronze Ramses statue from Egypt, a statue of Zenobia from Palmira (in ISIS-controlled Syria), you want to see a mummy? They bring it from Egypt when they have the revolution.' Tariq begins to catalogue other artefacts that he's seen pass through the wall. He describes rare and valuable artefacts pillaged from neighbouring Arab countries: early Bronze Age items from 3000BC, statues of important historical figures, including a Caesar's head from Libya, that have been looted during the chaos of the Arab Spring and quietly sold on to opportunistic Western buyers.

Tariq says he's seen it with his own eyes. He says that the Caesar's head was solid marble, a genuine piece of significant historical importance, but it was sold through an intermediary in Jerusalem to a buyer in the US for fifty thousand pounds and will probably never see the light of day again.

'The story is not about fakes any more,' says Tariq. Yes, there was a lucrative business in making fakes in workshops in nearby Lebanon or here in Palestine for sale to gullible tourists. But since the fall of Gaddafi and Mubarak and the rest of the Arab despots, a free-for-all antiquity grab has been going on. Under the cover of war, to the victor the spoils. And there's nobody prepared to police it. On the contrary, traders in Israel have been only too happy to aid and abet it.

How many pieces are we talking about?

Tariq says thousands.

Every year?

Every month.

But why don't the authorities intervene?

'Listen, here in Israel they consider it legal because the people bringing these items are dealers who own shops in Jerusalem and have certificates from the Israeli Antiquities Authority. So they buy these items from smugglers in Jordan, Syria, Egypt, and then they come to Jerusalem where they pay customs because they have permits from the Israeli Antiquities Authority. After that they can take it through Dubai or Abu Dhabi to London or New York.'

These revelations, if true, are shocking in the extreme. The historic cultural legacy of one of the oldest civilisations on the planet, stretching from Iraq in the east through Syria and Egypt all the way to Libya in the West is being openly plundered under the cover of political revolt. Whatever your politics, and however you feel about the individual claims for territory and power in the region, these items belong to its people. What is happening here is not so different to what the Nazis did during the Second World War.

Tariq is clearly not impressed with what is going on either. 'These bitches in Egypt, the first thing they did was go to raid the museum. I can now take you to a shop in Jerusalem where you can see artefacts from there. You can even see Egyptian mummies.'

I start to feel like my fake Roman cup pales into insignificance next to a looted Egyptian mummy. From what Tariq is saying, the market in fakes has been drowned out by the tidal wave of stolen genuine artefacts. What's the point in turning out trinkets from a workshop in Ramallah if you can make thousands smuggling the real thing out of the war zone next door? Presumably ISIS or whoever is plundering these art works is making their commission and so is everyone else involved in passing them along the chain. Once they reach Jerusalem, they can be packaged up and sold to greedy buyers in the West.

It's a sad situation. Much of the art stolen by the Nazis was eventually returned, due in large part to their fastidious record keeping. The big difference here is that ISIS are publicly destroying artefacts in Iraq, Syria and Libya. If these items are recorded as destroyed but in fact are smuggled out of the country and sold on the black market then what chance is there of ever recovering them?

Waled tells me that as it is getting dark, it is time to go. I must leave Tariq and head back across the wall while we still can. I thank Tariq for his time. I tell him that for my part, I will try to tell the story of what is happening. It seems like a tiny gesture but he shakes my hand. 'People must know. That is the only way to make it stop.' The court of public opinion is now the only hope for the Middle Eastern peoples' cultural legacy.

We drive back through the military checkpoints, stopping for the soldiers to check our papers and run their mirrors under our car looking for risks and threats and I wonder at the hypocrisy of it all. How could an airtight security system like this, designed to keep even the smallest incendiary devices out of Israel, allow something as large as an Egyptian mummy to pass through unless it was with someone's cooperation? If the flow of cultural artefacts is really passing to the West via Jerusalem, then somebody with influence must be facilitating it. Someone is being paid to look the other way.

I suppose it has always been this way. Since Spanish pirates brought barrels of brandy and port to the British coast under the cover of darkness back in the eighteenth century, smugglers have found ways to explain political systems for personal gain. If you build a wall then someone will find a way to sneak over it, and whatever they manage to bring with them will be more valuable because of it.

I leave Jerusalem with a genuine feeling of sadness because for all the individual triumph and suffering of discovering whether the antique you bought is a genuine hit or a worthless fake, I've uncovered something far more profound. When the fighting stops, where will the grandchildren of those fighting now find inspiration? Where will the great paintings and sculptures that can spur on the next generation of artists be found if these works have all been plundered and squirrelled off to private collections in the penthouses of New York and London? A whole region of the world has been robbed of its heritage, a region that will need that heritage more than most when it is finally ready to rebuild itself.

CHAPTER EIGHT

JOHNNY AND MARIELLA

'The devil lives on those tits'

ON ANY SCALE on international crime statistics, Colombia scores pretty high. It has six of the top fifty most violent cities in the world, a booming cocaine market controlled by some of the world's premier cartels, crippling poverty and fabulous wealth living side by side, violent paramilitary groups, widespread corruption and a roaring trade in kidnapping and extortion. And yet, it still manages to attract hundreds of thousands of foreign tourists every year. Most of whom arrive via the capital, Bogotá.

At first glance Bogotá doesn't seem a particularly touristic place; the altitude means the temperature rarely gets above mid-teens while proximity to the jungle and prevailing winds ensure it enjoys year-round cloud cover that reminds me of the years I spent living in the north of England. It's grey, it's pretty cold, and it's wet.

But because Bogotá has the biggest international airport in the region, most people end up spending a night or two here on their way to nicer parts of Colombia – the white sand beaches of the Caribbean coast for example.

So what does the average tourist do for a couple of days in Bogotá? Well, first up is La Candelaria, the city's old colonial district. Like many colonial towns in Latin America, this one comes complete with cobblestone streets, picturesque squares, churches and pretty pastel-coloured houses that date back to the days of the city's Spanish occupiers four hundred years ago. You can spend a very pleasant day wandering around La Candelaria's shops and cafes, enjoying the scenery and soaking up the atmosphere. If you have a little Spanish then you'll find that Colombian Spanish is a very refreshingly clean, crisp version of the language that falls very sympathetically indeed on the ears.

People in other parts of Latin America often remark about how Colombians are the friendliest folk on the continent and it shows when you step out of your hotel. Perhaps trying to undo the years of negative PR surrounding the country during the bad old days, Bogotá's residents are surprisingly forthcoming with helpful advice. You're never waiting long for a smile from a stranger in Bogotá.

I've arrived in Bogotá in July, which is pretty much peak season for European visitors. In the Candelaria district the quirky colourful cafes are full during the day and uptown, in Zona T, the neon and chrome-filled nightclubs and bars are pulling in the big weekend crowds. Unfortunately, this is where, for many visitors, the problems often start.

I'm here to investigate a disturbing recent phenomenon that I've heard started in Bogotá but is now
beginning to affect the whole country. In Colombia there
is an epidemic of date rape and robbery being facilitated
by the use of a drug called scopolamine.

Scopolamine (known as 'scope') is a date rape drug
usually administered to unsuspecting victims through their
drinks. What makes it different to many other similar drugs
is that the victim remains conscious but has no awareness
of what they are doing. It allegedly makes people suggestible to the point where they will willingly give up vital and
valuable personal information, such as their ATM PINs.
The side-effects are devastating, leaving victims in need
of hospitalisation. Some victims can take over a week to
come round. Use of the drug has reached epidemic proportions in Colombia; last year there were over fifty thousand
cases reported by Colombia's Ministry of the Interior. And
yet arrests for scopolamine-related crimes are rare.

A dark shadow has fallen over Bogotá. Tourists and
locals alike live under it, wondering whether the next
time they turn their back on their drink for a second,
they might be next.

I'm staying in a central Bogotá hotel just off Avenida
Jimenez. I'm excited to be here as this is my first time in
the country and I'm keen to take a look around. All I've
really ever read about Colombia has concerned FARC,

the Marxist peasant army who fund their rebellion through kidnap and ransom and cocaine distribution. But as I arrive here now, the news is that the rebels and the government are engaging in peace negotiations, which means all is quiet in the country.

I'm up bright and early for a light breakfast. After my pancakes, I decide to take a walk downtown. I want to get the lie of the land. It's a chilly morning and the sky is overcast and grey. The streets are busy with early morning commuter traffic and people fill the pavements milling around in every direction. Bogotá this morning feels like any other capital city during rush hour and, honestly, I feel like I could easily be anywhere.

Around two blocks from my hotel, a middle-aged guy wearing a pinstriped suit and a duffle coat walks up to me and gives a rather old-fashioned bow. 'Hello, sir, I am sorry to disturb you.' He's as polite as he is smartly presented in that old-fashioned way only guys of a certain age can pull off, hair slicked back with a bit of Brylcreem, shoes polished so you could see your face in them and a pencil-thin moustache that has been trimmed to within an inch of its life. After a few pleasant formalities, he gently enquires as to whether I might be interested in buying some emeralds today. I'm immediately on my guard, thinking to myself, 'Who in their right mind buys emeralds on the street?' But I decide to play along if only to see what he's up to.

The guy tells me his name is Heraldo and he pulls a small white envelope from his inside pocket, carefully unwrapping it to reveal around twenty-five small bright green stones. The largest is no bigger than my thumbnail. 'Esmereldas,' he says with a reassuring nod and invites me to take a closer look.

Now, I know next to nothing about emeralds but I'm intrigued enough to pick a few of the prettier ones out and give them a once over. I hold one up to the light and the bright green stone glows between my fingers. While I'm looking at the stones, we're joined by another four guys, all similar in age and appearance to Heraldo. One by one they produce their own white envelopes full of stones. There are large ones as well as wee little tiny ones. Each one of them implores me to take my time, it's all very polite and there's no hard sell.

How much? I have no idea what a rough emerald should cost. They talk me through it patiently explaining that the darker ones are worth more than the lighter ones, bigger is obviously better and I should look for obvious flaws because clearer stones are also worth more. The prices of these stones vary from the thousands for the larger and darker stones to thirty or forty dollars for smaller ones.

I'm slightly taken aback by their charm and the simplicity of their patter. There is no pushy sales pitch, no pressurising, no intimidation. In fact, there are none of the techniques that I've seen so many scam artists around the world employ in these situations to coerce a tourist into parting quickly with his cash. It's actually very informative. If I didn't know better, I'd say these guys were legit.

I'm curious enough to decide that I'll buy one of the cheaper ones. Maybe I can find an expert later to check it out. Maybe this is some kind of rip-off. I didn't come to Bogotá looking for a gemstone scam but I figure you should never look a gift horse in the mouth.

By now there are nearly twenty guys gathered around and offering stones. I decide to stick with Heraldo; I like his polite little bows and his formality. I pick out a small stone about half the width of my little finger-nail and Heraldo and I enjoy a little laugh together as we haggle over the price. Eventually we agree that I'll pay Heraldo seventy dollars for his emerald. Maybe I'm being ripped off but we part on good terms and I have my first contact in Bogotá.

On my way back to the hotel, I notice a row of legitimate jewellery stores. The windows are full of rings and necklaces with price tags just like you'd see back home. I wonder if I can get my new purchase valued. I pick out a shop that turns out to be owned by an American. Lee Wasson is a US jeweller who has been working in Bogotá for over forty years. He's a tall, bald Southerner with a hangdog face and talks with a slow confident drawl. I ask him if he wouldn't mind having a look at the stone I bought on the street.

Lee takes me up to his office on the sixth floor. It's a pretty spectacular view of the city as the room has windows on three sides. As we sit down at Lee's big hardwood desk he explains it's important to have as much natural light as possible when looking at gemstones.

I explain to Lee what just happened out on the street with Heraldo and ask if he'd give me his honest assessment. I give him my new emerald and watch as, with a pair of tweezers in one hand and a jeweller's eyeglass in the other, he starts to carefully analyse the stone. 'Not bad,' he says, turning the stone over. 'Okay colour, minor inclusions, probably weighs about fifty points.'

'Is it a fake?' I ask.

'No. It's a real emerald. I'd probably pay around fifty dollars for it if I went down to the market.'

I tell Lee that I paid seventy and he nods. 'Yeah, well, they don't know you, so you probably paid a little extra.'

He says that the market has been there on Jimenez for a long long time and the reason it's on the street isn't that the dealers are small-time pedlars but rather that, for the same reason Lee's office has so many windows, the only light an emerald dealer will trust is natural sunlight.

'Most of the guys down in the market are pretty straight,' says Lee. 'But there are less scrupulous operators too. Sometimes guys will try to pass off fake emeralds to customers who don't know better, but the genuine dealers tend to push them out pretty quickly. They look at those guys as parasites, bad for business.'

I thank Lee for his time and his opinion. I'm a bit surprised that the emerald turned out to be real and even a little disappointed. I thought I may have inadvertently stumbled into a gemstone scam, which would have been something new and interesting for me to investigate, but instead I've got a fifty-dollar souvenir from Colombia.

Tonight I'm going to hit the town in search of some evidence of the scope gangs I've read about. Most newspaper reports suggest that tourists drinking in the trendy new uptown bars around Zona T have been particularly vulnerable and so that's where I'm heading. I'm dressed up smart so that anyone sizing me up would easily mistake me for a guy with plenty of money.

As I sit in the cab heading up the Avenida Carrera 14, I chat with my driver, a bald middle-aged guy called Juan who says he's been driving cabs in the city for most of his life. Juan says when he's not working he likes to travel and he's spent a lot of time working his way around the Americas, even living for two years in New York at one point. 'New York has its own problems,' he explains, 'but nothing like here. Here the big problem for us and for the tourists is the scopolamine.' He shakes his head at me in the mirror and tuts. 'They can put it in your drink, they can even blow it in your face. I know taxi drivers who've been drugged like that. And once you're under, then there is no escape, they will rob you until all your money is gone from your bank account and then they'll throw you out into the street.' He seems really sad about it.

Juan drops me off along a busy street in Zona T, which has brightly lit bars on either side of the road. I have a quick scan of what's around and again I'm surprised at how similar it all is to other Western cities. There's very little that says Colombia. There's the usual mix of faux Irish pubs and glitzy-looking techno bars that every modern city in the world seems to have these days. Young people fill the streets, crawling their way from bar to bar. It's only 9 p.m. but there are already signs of drunkenness. I have a sense of being in the wrong place, which of course means the right place for what I'm looking for. 'Be careful, my friend,' says Juan with a genuine concern as he hands me my change.

I've arranged to meet with a British journalist I know called Carl (not his real name) who lives in town. He's picked the Irish bar as a meeting point for us, maybe on the basis that familiar surroundings might comfort me, given the risk I'm about to take. He's waiting for me at an outdoor table. Carl's been living here for a few years working as a stringer for British newspapers.

His knowledge of the city is pretty good, his Spanish is excellent, but he's the perfect wingman for me because he's a Gringo. We need to come up with a plan so that we can flush out a scopolamine predator without actually ending up in a Colombian hospital ward.

After a bit of a brainstorm we come up with a strategy we think can work.

I move inside and sit up at the bar on a stool where I order a glass of beer, take two large sips and wait for Carl to take a seat on the other side of the bar. Nobody seeing us would ever guess we knew each other. Carl is wearing a dark baseball cap. Our code is that should he see anyone tamper with my drink then he is to turn his cap around. In the event that should happen then we move to stage two of the plan. But until then we need to flush out a 'scoper'. Once we're settled, I take another sip of my beer and then leave it unattended while I head off to the toilet. Now I have to trust Carl to keep an eye on my drink.

Unfortunately when I return, Carl's cap is still on the right way. Nobody has been near my drink. In a city of 8 million, this feels a little like looking for a needle in a haystack but by dressing smart, ordering my drinks in English and then leaving them unattended while I go to the toilet, I'm doing everything I can to shorten the odds. We try again another couple of times but, without any bites, we decide to move to another bar across the street.

This time I position myself next to a group of Colombian girls at the long bar. The PA is playing loud mid-Atlantic derivative pop music and the vibe inside is plastic and pointless. I order another beer and wait for Carl to get into place. Once I can see he's found a seat where he has a clear view of my drink, I take off to the toilet again and give it a good five minutes; plenty of time for someone to slip something into my glass. Alas, again the cap is still on when I get back. It doesn't look like this is going to be my night.

We move again a couple of times but only to draw another couple of blanks. We decide to try again tomorrow. Carl and I say good night and I head back to my hotel, a little tipsy but still very conscious. I'm not sure whether to be disappointed or relieved.

I've wrestled with the potential consequences of what I'm attempting to do. What if my drink gets spiked at a moment when Carl doesn't have a clear view of my drink? What if, for reasons beyond our control, I end up taking a hit of scope? The prognosis isn't good.

In a bar round the corner from my hotel I meet up with a young man who Carl has arranged for me to talk to about his own scopolamine experience. He's still embarrassed about what happened so he wants to keep his name a secret but twelve months ago he was out with a group of friends when he met what he describes as a 'super hot' girl. He told his friends to carry on without him, he told them he'd pulled. He acknowledges that shortly after his friends had left, he felt unusually drunk. 'I thought it was just the drink,' he says. 'But no. The next thing I know it's five days later and I'm in the hospital.'

Everything he owned had been robbed in the meantime. His two bank accounts had been emptied and the scopers had even visited his flat and stolen laptops and jewellery. 'After three days the police found me by the side of the street, no shirt, no shoes, screaming like a madman.'

It took another two days in hospital before he regained any control of his thoughts. 'I still have panic attacks. I'm afraid to go out. And now I carry a Picana.' He pulls a high-voltage cattle prod from his pocket. 'I'm not going to let anyone get on top of me again.'

The paranoia in his eyes is evident. He's a young man whose life has been irreparably damaged by the scopolamine experience.

The scope gangs only operate at night so I'm going to fill my time during the day seeing what more I can find out about emeralds. In particular, I'd love to see the 'parasites' Lee told me about. I put on my smartest tourist garb and walk back down Avenida Jimenez. A block before where Heraldo and the other dealers hang out there's another large square full of guys of a similar age to Heraldo but much less smartly dressed. I approach one of them and ask if he is selling 'esmereldas'.

The guy is older than Heraldo, maybe mid-sixties. His hair is slicked back with some oil and he has a large pair of tortoise-shelled glasses on the end of his big bulbous nose. Over his faded brown suit, he's wearing a grey anorak from which he pulls the white envelope. There's something in his demeanour that is quite different to Heraldo, more shifty, he keeps looking around to check if anyone is watching. He has none of Heraldo's confidence and charm.

He gets my attention when I see the size of the gems he's offering. They're huge. Bigger than an almond. From what I learned yesterday, these stones should cost tens of thousands of dollars. But this guy, who says his name is Guillermo, is asking for a mere three hundred dollars. I chuckle a little when he says it, which he must mistake for a bit of haggling because he drops the price to one hundred! These rocks can't be the real thing. They have to be fake.

I hold up the four-carat 'emerald' Guillermo is now offering me for a hundred dollars and tell him I know it's a fake.

'No, no,' he says with his arms outstretched and his palms plaintively open to the skies. 'It's real, it's a real one.'

I'm no gemstone expert but even I can see the flaws. I point out a join where it looks like two pieces of glass have been glued together. 'Come on,' I tell him. 'Where do you get these from? Tell me and I'll buy them all.'

I've got his attention now. I explain to him that I'm not police. I come up with a cover story that I'm potentially in the market to buy a whole load of fake stones if the price is right. And in return as my contact, I tell him there might even be a slice of the pie for him too. 'How much?' he asks. Gotcha. Now we're talking on the level. 'Ten per cent,' I say. Standard. But only if I can meet the man behind the fakes. I'll only do the final deal face to face. No middlemen.

Guillermo is now looking around the square again to see who is watching us. I can see his beady little eyes flicking around, all the while running the numbers in his head for what I might be worth. 'I need to make some calls,' he says. 'There is someone I can call but he doesn't know you. I'll need to speak with him first and explain what you want. This is not a good business. You know?'

Suddenly, while Guillermo is still talking, there is a commotion in the square. There is a sound of gunshots and then screaming as people begin running both ways up and down the street. Moments later, the air is filled with the sound of ambulances and police sirens. This is officially a situation. Another guy who must know Guillermo comes up to us. 'Someone has been shot at the market,' he says and runs off.

Guillermo looks concerned. 'You see? This is not a good business,' he repeats. We exchange numbers quickly and Guillermo takes off across the square. I head the other way to see if I can find out any more but already the police are cordoning off the street with tape and the crowd is four deep.

The next morning I take a coffee on the terrace outside my hotel and read the morning papers. The headline reads 'Emerald Dealer Killed in Town Centre'. Pedro Ortegon, a sixty-four-year-old emerald dealer with links to the Medellin Cartel, was assassinated by a sixteen-year-old kid (already in custody) who claims he was paid 5 million pesos to carry out a hit. The shooting happened in the exact spot where I was speaking to Heraldo the day before. The paper speculates that since the death from cancer a couple of months ago of the so-called Emerald Tsar, the unofficial boss of the market, a power vacuum has opened up, which certain people are prepared to go to extreme lengths to fill.

I run thorough the 'what ifs'. Particularly the 'what if the hit had been organised for twenty-four hours earlier?' What if I'd bumped into Guillermo further along the road? What if I'd been caught up in the crossfire? Lee spoke about the emerald market as though it was a safe old establishment, part of the city's culture, but nobody mentioned cartels or organised assassinations and mafia power battles. It seems the Colombia I'd read about before coming here, with all the drugs and guns, is still alive and well.

That evening I get a call from Guillermo. The meet with the guy who makes the fakes is on but his contact is very nervous since the shooting so he suggests we meet in a bar downtown at 9 p.m. From the sound of his voice, he doesn't seem confident and I get a sense that there might still be a fair amount of convincing to be done. I'll have to be on my best behaviour.

At 8.45 p.m. I hop in a cab but the driver looks a little surprised when I tell him the address. I'm tempted to ask him why but have a feeling it's not going to be something I want to hear. When we eventually pull off the main road into a busy side street, I begin to realise exactly what kind of district we're in. This is not on the tourist trail; in fact, I doubt even most Bogotá residents would be seen dead in this place.

The doorman is packing a Glock 17. I can see it sticking out from under his jacket as he pats me down. Where I come from, seeing a gun is a rare thing and always makes me feel a little uneasy. Happy that I'm unarmed, he moves aside and allows me to pass into a narrow stairway. There's a long smoky mirror running up the wall. I check myself out as I climb the stairs – jeans, leather jacket – at home I'd say I looked like an undercover cop but round here, who knows? Probably just another dumb Gringo who's wandered into the wrong part of town.

Guillermo has instructed me to wait at the bar. He says his contact has my description and will find me. The place is neck deep in loud gassy music, a mixture of Latino and American. There's a handful of people dancing in the middle of the room but the majority are sitting at low tables necking beers and rum. I'm the only Gringo. It's Friday night and everyone wants to get loaded, to put the troubles of the week out of their minds for another weekend.

The bar is in the corner of the room. It's about ten feet long, two girls running it. The first girl spends her time cracking open bottles of Aguila. She carefully decants each one into a plastic cup, which the second girl runs out to the people sitting at tables. This is the same kind of safety strategy they employ at British football grounds to stop opposing fans smashing bottles over each other. I order a cerveza for myself and prop up the bar.

After half an hour waiting as instructed, there's still no sign of Guillermo or his contact, I'd say someone is having second thoughts. I'm not exactly surprised. It's natural that he'll suspect that I'm police or worse, working for the insurance companies. They routinely send their own investigators to Colombia to uncover fake gemstone rackets.

I step outside to get away from the music and call Guillermo but his phone is turned off. On my way back to the bar, the barmaid comes walking towards me. Something is up. She takes me by the arm and leans in close to shout over the bass. 'Watch out!' Her breath feels hot on my ear. 'The girl standing at the bar has put something in your drink. It's not good for you to stay here.'

Now, this is a turn up for the books.

I thank the barmaid but I reassure her that I'm on top of it. No need to worry. Then I head back over and smile at a girl propping up the bar next to my unattended drink. I have to think quick. Start up a conversation with her. I tell her I'm waiting for my friend but it doesn't look as though he's going to turn up. She nods. Seems disinterested. She's sucking beer through a straw straight from the bottle. We engage in some clunky small talk. My barroom Spanish is stretched to the max. She's starting to look impatient and every minute or so she glances down towards my glass. I decide to make a play. I swig the whole remaining half glass of beer down in one. But like Monica Lewinsky, I don't swallow. Instead I motion to my new girlfriend that I need to take a leak and in the dim light of the bar, I'm pretty sure she hasn't spotted that my mouth is still full of beer.

Inside the bathroom, I spit the poisoned beer into the sink and immediately rinse my mouth out with water half-a-dozen times. From what I've heard about scope, even a small dose can leave you as suggestible as a teenage boy with a hard on at a convent school disco. But reassured that I've gotten rid of the last dregs, I text Carl and ask him to meet me at my hotel room in half an hour. After that, I head back out to the bar. It's time to show my acting chops. I need this girl to believe that I'm drugged and ready for whatever she has planned.

When I get to the bar, I order a fresh beer for both of us and she suggests we take a turn around the dance floor. Why not? We glide together over the tiles to the melodious rhythms of Justin Timberlake and I tell her I'm not sure if it's the music or not but I'm suddenly feeling a little light-headed. I suggest we take a walk. She sees my 'walk' and raises me a 'Why don't we just go back to your hotel room?' My mother warned me about girls like this.

The taxi turns up right away and in no time we're heading back uptown towards my hotel. I keep up the drunk act while Mariella (not her real name, or maybe it is) starts to tell me how handsome I am. Even with my limited Spanish, I can tell something isn't right. I tip the driver at the hotel and we're straight past the concierge, into the lift and up to my room in five seconds flat. Mariella makes herself comfortable on the sofa in the room and asks me to put some music on. She's watching me like a hawk, presumably waiting for me to keel.

It's unusual being preyed on like this by a woman. The majority of criminals I have encountered have been men. I wonder if she's operating alone or what kind of guy might be backing her up and whether he's waiting at the end of a phone somewhere for Mariella's call.

I get a text from Carl to say he's in the lobby downstairs. I tell him to grab the concierge, come up quietly and guard my door. I don't want anyone to go in or out until I've spoken to Mariella.

I take a seat right next to her on the sofa. I drop the drunk act like a stone and straight out ask her, 'What was in the drink?' No sense in beating around the bush with a woman who is trying to drug you.

Now it's Mariella's turn to act. She immediately starts to feign ignorance. She's no Meryl Streep. There's a reason she's turning tricks in a Bogotá bar and not winning an Oscar.

I can't stand to watch it. I interrupt the performance and just tell her that I know she drugged my drink in the bar, that the bar girl saw her put something in my glass while I was outside on the phone. I suspect she's probably working with someone else and I say I want to meet him. She starts to get a little nervous and begins to pack up her stuff. She's flustered and gabbling a little that she doesn't know what I'm talking about, that I'm a crazy Gringo. She opens the hotel room door and nearly jumps out of her skin when she sees Carl, the concierge and a security guy standing right behind it. I gently take her by the elbow and suggest that she sit back down. Nobody is going anywhere until we all have a little chat.

Mariella begins to cry. I can't tell if this is genuine shock or part of a routine. But it unsettles me. Up until now, I hadn't ever felt like I was the bad guy but I have to admit that I do feel a little uneasy that I am forcing her to stay here when I can see she'd much rather run away. I try to keep my voice calm to reassure her that she's not in any trouble and she's certainly not in any danger. I tell her I'm not with the police and I'm not going to get them involved, I just want some answers. First of which is 'What was in the drink?'

She stops crying for just long enough to look me dead in the eye. I can tell she's weighing up her options like a toddler who stops mid-tantrum to see what flavour peace offering you have. I open my arms and give her the most unthreatening and trustworthy look I can muster. 'Burundanga,' she says carefully.

'And what was going to happen if I'd really drunk it?' I ask.

'You would have fallen asleep. And I would have called Johnny. He's waiting in a car across the street,' she says. Whoever Johnny is, he must have been following us all the way back from the club.

I explain to Mariella that I'm cool with all of this. No harm done. But I really want to talk to Johnny. If we can clear this up then everyone can go home. Mariella gets upset again, maybe she's worried that she'll get in trouble but that's really not my problem and besides, I'm confident we'll all go home happy in the end. Reluctantly she calls a number on her cell and turns on the waterworks again. 'Johnny,' she blubs, 'Johnny, come quickly, it's gone bad Johnny, I'm scared Johnny. Come quickly now.' She gives Johnny the room number and looks back to me for approval.

I feel sorry for Mariella. There's a thin line between perpetrator and victim sometimes and I think Mariella is a good example of a girl who has ended up in bad company. I wonder what she would be doing if she wasn't doing this. Of course, it's possible that maybe she simply chose this life but somehow I doubt it. I imagine for a girl like Mariella, the choices were limited and Johnny offered her a way to live. I guess I'm about to find out more when he arrives.

I go and explain to the boys outside the door that there's a guy coming up. The concierge wants to call the cops right away but I convince him to wait. I try to reassure him, this is better for everyone if we can sort it out ourselves. Not the kind of publicity the hotel needs for sure. A minute later, a short skinny guy in his late twenties gets out of the lift. I expected him to be a bit spooked at the sight of four guys waiting in the corridor for him but he swaggers up to us bold as brass. 'Where's the girl?'

I ask him to follow me back into the room.

Johnny is high. Very high. I can feel his body heat from three feet away and his breathing is shallow and erratic. There is no fear in this guy's eyes. The corners of his mouth keep twitching erratically and I swear he seems to be enjoying himself. We sit on the sofa next to Mariella and I pour him a beer. Then I bring him up to speed with what Mariella has already told me. He nods. Yes, he confirms all of this is true. He says that the plan was that once I was asleep, she would let him into the room and together they would steal everything they could get their hands on. 'Your laptop, your passport, your phone. All the things I can sell.'

I'm curious about the drug. I'd heard that scope made its victims suggestible but not unconscious. 'Yes, you're right,' he says. 'But this is not scope. This drug is Ativan, it's more like a sedative, like Rohypnol. It just knocks you out. There are people in Bogotá who use scope like you say but these are much worse people than me. You can kill people with scope. I don't want to kill anyone.'

And Mariella? I'm interested to know how long has she been involved in this little racket. 'She's nineteen. I've been working her for around eighteen months now.'

Mariella's shame is there for us all to see. Johnny looks at her but she can't return eye contact. She stares down at the floor, her tears falling onto her bare legs.

Johnny looks at me again and says it's time to go. It's another one of those strange moments that my life seems full of at the moment where I'm grateful to the same people who are trying to hurt me. I can intellectualise it but emotionally it still feels a little upsetting.

Johnny isn't at all threatening. He even says that he can make some enquiries. There's a guy he knows who works with a scope gang. He seems cool with me and he shakes my hand with his warm, limp, damp hand as he leaves. 'Thanks for being cool about all this,' he says with a shrug. And then taking Mariella by the hand he leaves. I have an idea, so I run after him.

'Tell the guy I'm in the market to buy some scope. And I'm paying cash.'

He nods. Okay.

Santa Fe is the red-light district of Bogotá. It's where all the hookers and dealers hang out to hook and deal. The walls are covered head to toe with Bogotá's characteristic street graffiti. Images of twenty-foot-high golden eagles blend seamlessly with coded numbers delineating turf. Boys on motorbikes whizz around while girls in skimpy vest tops and miniskirts desperately try to catch the eye of potential customers.

I arrive at the address Johnny gave me, a nightclub in the centre of the district. It's still only six o'clock so it's getting dark but there's no clientele here yet. I push open a large steel security door and poke my head inside. 'Hola,' I call into the empty corridor.

'Inside,' comes the reply.

Down the hall is a fairly standard bar/nightclub. The lower ground floor is around one hundred square metres, open plan, concrete floor, a long bar along one wall. There are beer taps along the front and 376 different types of rum stacked up on shelves behind. The bartender's quietly slicing a thousand limes in the corner. He pays me no attention. The man I assume I've come to see is sitting alone smoking a cigarette at a table near the centre of the room.

Fernando owns the club. He's tall for a Colombian, maybe five foot ten, thickset and his eyebrows hang heavily on his brow so that he looks like he's permanently frowning. He has the regulation tattooed forearms that gangsters in this part of the world always have and a couple of gold teeth finish off the look. But the unique thing I notice about him as I shake his hand is the unmistakable smell of semen on his breath. Fresh, hot, spunky breath. I wasn't expecting that. As there's only the three of us in here, I'm wondering if the bartender was the lucky guy.

Johnny has given Fernando a heads up already so I tell him what I want. I want to buy a hundred grams of scopolamine, enough for twenty doses.

'This is better for you.' He tries to fob me off with some Ativan. He says it's a better alternative, 'Much safer. People can die on scopolamine if you get the dose wrong. With Ativan they just pass out.'

But I tell him I want the scope because it has the benefits I'm looking for. He thinks about it for a moment. 'Okay,' he consents. And switches the Ativan for a small bag of white powder.

Now we've broken the ice, I ask him what's his preferred method. In alcohol? 'Put it in their drink. If they're not drinking alcohol then you put it in their juice or water. You have to be careful with the dose or you can kill people.'

Something crosses his mind and he chuckles to himself. What's the joke? 'I have this one woman, she works for me. She puts it on her tits and gets the guy to snort it off by telling him that it's coke. She has Danadas.' In Colombia, Danadas is the word pimps use for surgically enhanced breasts, literally it means 'damaged'. 'The devil lives on those tits.' He laughs. 'Be very careful. In Colombia. Don't get close to anyone. All over Colombia, everywhere there is evil.'

I'm interested in how people come to work for him. He has a crew who he calls his 'Eagles.' Every night of the weekend they go out on the hunt. They are three women, two men and two trans. 'They are all very good-looking.' He seems proud of them. 'And when they find someone, someone who is looking good, a tourist like you maybe, then they strike. They can charm even you.'

Fernando says the trick for an 'Eagle' is to win your trust. When they have that, they can easily slip a dose of scope into your drink and within fifteen minutes, you're that drunk guy in the bar that has to be helped out by your 'friend' to the taxi. We've all seen that guy. Many of us have been that guy so nobody else in the bar suspects for a second that there's anything untoward going on. But you better hope to God that you're not that guy in this case because your new friend isn't taking you home, but rather to Fernando's club. Where he has a very special room prepared for you.

Upstairs, above the bar is the dance floor. It's a mezzanine level about half the size of the bar below, turntables and speakers in one corner, probably big enough to hold around a hundred and fifty people dancing. Tucked away in one corner is the toilet and next to that a door that looks like it might be the cleaning cupboard. Fernando unlocks the door and I can see right away that there's no mop and bucket inside. It's a tiny room with a filthy stained mattress on the floor. There's a window but it's heavily fortified with metal bars. This is a cell. Somewhere for people to be held against their will.

Fernando explains. Once his Eagles find a target, they bring them back to the club and place them in this room. 'Two or three days here is normal,' says Fernando. 'But it depends on how much money they have. Once you have them here and they have taken scopolamine they give you the ATM numbers.'

Is it that simple? I ask. I mean do you still have to apply a bit of pressure?

'No.' Fernando holds up a finger. 'Nothing. You say, "Hey, let's get some money for some drinks, give me your ATM cards and the number and I'll go and get the money." And they just do it.'

It sends a chill down my spine to hear him say it. This is a drug that makes you incredibly vulnerable, exposed to the power of whoever you come into contact with, and I feel like the last person I'd want that to be is Fernando and the last place is here in his private cell.

'So while one of you is at the bank emptying this person's account, what's happening to them in here?' I ask.

Fernando gives me a dark look. 'You keep them happy. Some cocaine, some drinks. You have a good time. You know?' He's alluding to something so strongly I have to ask.

'Sex?'

He nods and a dark, gold-toothed, spunky smile slides across his mouth. That's when I realise the full horror of this room. You remain locked in this room for days on end, kept topped up with drugs and drinks, and while all your worldly wealth is being slowly milked from your private bank accounts, you are being simultaneously raped in this small filthy dungeon, perfectly situated next to a noisy dance floor where the music and cheering of the crowd will drown out your screams.

'While one person is doing that, the other person is out at the ATM machine taking all the money out. You need to go slowly. If you give them all the drugs at the same time then they'll pass out. You need to keep doing it until they have nothing left. When you're ready to get rid of them then you put them in a taxi and get them out of this zone.'

And that's it. The next thing a scopolamine victim knows, like the guy I met in the bar, they're in hospital with days missing from their memory, no money left in the world and the fallout of serious sexual abuse, often including an STD. And as I've already heard, the psychological trauma is even more profound and long-lasting.

I ask Fernando when someone was last in this room. He says it was eight days ago. He and one of his Eagles held a man in here for four days while they took everything from his bank and home. 'We made around three thousand dollars plus a laptop, phone and some jewellery.' Afterwards they dumped the man in the street.

'Do you enjoy your job?' I ask him.

'It's not that I enjoy it.' Then he shrugs. 'It's just the only option that I have at the moment.'

'What makes a person good at this job?'.

'You have to be very cunning,' he says. 'And you have to know what you're going to do and how.'

'And you?' I ask. 'Are you cunning?'

He gives the loudest laugh. A real belly laugh that throws his head backwards. 'Yes. I am very cunning.'

I don't doubt it for a second. Fernando seems extremely professional. He says his club is doing good business. The scope work is just to make some 'money on the side'. Although tourists make easy targets, Fernando says that he picks up locals too. Anyone who looks like they have money and can be manipulated into taking the drug is fair game as far as he's concerned. It's incredible that despite everyone I've met since I arrived in Bogotá warning me about scopolamine, it still goes on on such a grand scale. Fernando says it is because people are careless when they drink. That's what he preys upon.

I think Fernando is the closest thing to evil that I've encountered on my travels. He's a genuine monster. He shows no remorse and he seems not to care in the least how his victims end up. He describes himself as a 'hedonist' because his motivation is to enjoy himself but he doesn't mind if that comes at the cost of someone else's savings or indeed their sanity. Being with him makes me feel sick to my stomach and it makes me wonder whether I should turn him over to the authorities. But I know I won't.

Most of the people in this book behave immorally. That fact is in no doubt. However, in order to do my job, I often have to reserve that judgement. I cannot wag an admonishing finger at someone and at the same time expect them to open up to me about their life. I cannot ask for someone's time and honesty and not pay them the same respect that I would anyone else. This may strike some as odd, but I see my role as someone who brings stories to light so that others who hear them can be forewarned. I want people to have the information they need to protect themselves against the worst. Fernando is a clear example of this. I could shop Fernando to the cops and he might be arrested. He might not. I have no evidence, bar his testimony, and I have no idea what officials he might have in his pocket. Colombia's police force is notoriously corrupt. But that's not really the point. I have only been able to write this book because people like Fernando have been generous enough with their time and honest enough about themselves to make it possible. As much as it disgusts me to do so I have to thank him and indeed that is what I do before I leave. I thank the serial rapist for his time and I leave.

Now as I write this I feel the revulsion all over again. I have had nightmares about Fernando's private cell and I run the arguments over and over in my head, I suppose because I am still troubled by my own logic. And yet, I still think I have made the right decision. If the official figures are to be believed, there are hundreds of Fernandos operating in Colombia and I pray that you, now reading this, will have been affected enough by what you have read to never leave your drink unattended ever again. If this has effected such a change in you then perhaps it has in others. Because my decision only makes sense to me as long as I feel that that means more people have been saved from falling foul of a scopolamine gang than could have been by simply having Fernando investigated by the police.

As I leave Colombia and head home, I wonder whether I will ever return. I have not fallen in love with this place as I have with other places I have visited. I have met charming people like Heraldo and Juan, but I feel a heaviness in Bogotá that I think belies a place that still bears the scars of its troubled past. Maybe one day I'll come back but I don't think it will be any time soon.

CHAPTER NINE

SHAKY GROUND

'Sorry. It's my problem'

I COULDN'T FINISH this book without including a taste of home. I love London. That's why I live here. But I want to see if I can find its seedy underbelly. I'm starting to wonder whether there are some scams that emerge simply because the environment is right for them. Scopolamine or secuestro express work well in Latin America, but don't feel like they would fly for long if the criminals in London were to try it here. I wonder if there is simply a sort of natural emergence for scams in any given environment? And if so, what kind of crimes is London particularly good for? What kind of opportunities are there for predatory criminals in my city to prey on?

London welcomes over 15 million international visitors every year, making it one of the 'big three' destinations globally. It also has a huge British influx. Daily, millions of people commute into the city to work. The pace is fast. People move quickly and they don't stop unless it's absolutely necessary. When I first moved here

I felt exhausted for the first few weeks just from getting around never mind all the other things I had to do.

When people visit London they often complain that the people aren't friendly. That isn't my experience of the city. I think people will help you out but you have to ask for it. Otherwise they're likely to just pass by without noticing. Sorry. In a rush. You know how it is.

All this makes London an easy place to be invisible. I'm optimistic as I begin my search that there are criminals here, who maybe live right under my nose but who I just haven't noticed before. I want to slow down and take a closer look – open my eyes and see if there's a side of the city that I've never seen before.

I've decided to start by investigating one of the city's growth industries. Every day, it seems, the press reports on the epidemic of mobile phone theft. If you believe the papers, there's a typhoon of theft rampaging through the city. The problem must be pretty bad here because I've noticed of late that some bar staff have taken to wearing T-shirts with logos that ask customers, 'Do You Know Where Your Phone Is?'

My strategy is to use a contact of mine who I've worked with many times before. Saul (he doesn't want me to use his real name) is a 'fixer', which means he has a Rolodex of contacts around the world. I asked him if he had connections to the kind of people who stole phones in London and wasn't really surprised to hear that he had. We've come up with a way to explore the phenomenon by setting a little trap.

I'm going to use myself as bait in order to see how the thief operates. The trick is that Saul and I are in on it. But the thief is in the dark. Saul has set him up. He's told the guy that I'm an easy target and that he has his own reasons for wanting to see me get robbed. Said it was a revenge kind of thing. Either way, he's not asked too many questions. In return, the thief has been told that he can keep whatever he gets. The crucial thing, from my point of view, is that the guy has no idea that Saul and I are friends. As far as he's concerned, I'm a genuine victim.

One of his favourite areas to work in is Hoxton Square just next to Shoreditch. In the last five years, the East End of London has exploded and become the city's social centre. Much of the nightlife that was once centred on central districts such as Soho and Covent Garden has moved east to Hoxton and Shoreditch. Crime statistics published by London's Metropolitan Police suggest that the criminals have followed the herd. And so I've picked a sunny spot outside a cafe in Hoxton with an iPhone prominently displayed for all to see on the table in front of me.

I sit for an hour outside the cafe. It's Friday evening and the bars and clubs around the square are beginning to fill up. There's a genuine buzz around the place. A group of girls sitting at the table next to me have ordered a bottle of white wine and I can catch snippets of the stories they're telling each other about the week they've had.

It's the usual deal for a Friday night. A couple of times someone comes over to ask me for a light or if they can take a look at the menu on my table. Each time I brace myself in case this is the thief I've been waiting for, but each time I'm a little disappointed to discover that my phone is still on the table. Then a young Indian guy comes over and sits down opposite me.

'Don't I know you?' he asks.

'I don't think so,' I say. It's possible, of course, that he's seen me on TV, it happens every now and again.

'I do,' he says. 'I definitely recognise you.' He smiles as though he's worked it out. He has a heavy Indian accent and I wonder whether he's going to ask me if I know someone that he knows. But then out of nowhere another guy, dressed in black, hood pulled up, eyes down, runs along the street, leans over the table, snatches the iPhone off the table and runs as fast as he can in the opposite direction.

Despite the fact that I've been waiting for this exact moment to happen, I freeze a little. I was so distracted by the Indian guy who is already getting up to walk off. I jump up to chase after the runner but the Indian guy blocks me off. 'No,' he says. 'Sorry, I think I was thinking you were someone else.' And he walks away.

I have to think for a moment. These guys are clearly working together. But I'm not 100 per cent sure they're Saul's contact. The Indian guy is walking away from me, casually back up the street, and my phone is gone. My plan was to try to follow on foot but then I hadn't figured on there being two of them. So I grab a napkin off the table and scribble down my actual phone number (my real phone is still safely in my pocket), run after the Indian guy and hand him the napkin.

He looks at the napkin. 'Just take it,' I say. 'I know you and that guy are working together. Call this number and you can keep the phone, I just want to talk to you.'

The guy starts shaking his head and he tries to hand the napkin back to me. 'Fuck off, man,' he says. 'I don't know that guy.'

I'm tempted to mention Saul but I don't want to blow cover. I want him to continue to think I'm just another ordinary victim. 'It's fine,' I say. 'I don't care about the phone. Keep it. And if you call this number and meet up with me, then I'll make it worth your while.'

My hunch is that these guys are part of a gang. With thousands of phones going missing in London every year, I have a feeling that the business must be coordinated. Someone is getting rich off the back of it. These two guys are in all likelihood only foot soldiers. But if I can get in with them, then I can work my way up the chain. The Indian guy keeps shaking his head and protesting his innocence but, with a bit of pressure, he takes the napkin. He puts it in his pocket as he walks away.

I run back to the cafe and take my laptop out of my bag. I'm interested to see if it's possible to track the phone using the software on my laptop. I load it up and, right away, I can see from the green dot on the screen that my phone is online and heading up the Kingsland Road. It looks as though the thief is heading towards Dalston, about half a mile away. I engage the 'lost iPhone' feature, which locks the phone remotely. Then I pay up and head as fast as I can towards Dalston.

Dalston is an area of East London that is said to be 'on the up'. The cool kids, priced out of Shoreditch, have begun to move in looking for cheaper housing. There's already evidence of gentrification: bearded hipsters on fixed geared bikes and punky girls with bright blue hair. But Dalston is also still a deprived area and crime rates are sky high. For now, the area hangs on to its community but the clock is ticking for the fried chicken restaurants and thrift stores. And, as with most suburban shopping areas in British cities, there's no shortage of second-hand phone shops.

I log in to my online account and look again for my stolen phone. The green dot has gone. The message that tells me my phone is now offline. By now the thieves have almost certainly removed the SIM card from the phone and wiped the handset. Odds on that my phone is already for sale in one of these second-hand phone shops along Kingsland Road. I count half-a-dozen phone shops along the half-mile stretch and decide I'll try each one.

The first shop is really no more than a hole-in-the-wall kiosk. There's an Indian guy behind the counter with a glass cabinet full of second-hand smartphones. Above his head is an LED sign that reads 'We Unlock and Repair iPhones'. I ask the guy if he has any phones for sale that match the one I just had stolen. He shakes his head. Not today. I ask if he buys second-hand phones. 'Yes of course,' he says. 'But only if you have ID.'

I wonder how much he would pay for a phone like the one I had stolen.

'Depends on the condition,' he says. 'But one hundred and fifty to two hundred pounds.'

I work my way up the street going into each phone shop along the way. They're all remarkably similar. None of them have my phone. At least none of them are advertising it, so I head home to see if my phone has come back online. Of course it hasn't.

Saul has a friend who used to work for the Metropolitan Police. Now he does bits of security and investigation work for TV companies. Sid's a proper geezer, cockney to his core, the kind of old-fashioned London copper that you don't see much these days. His hair is cropped close to his head and his skin is thick as leather. He's missing two of his front teeth and he smokes rolled-up cigarettes right down to his dirty yellow fingers. Sid laughs his head off when I tell him the story of what happened to my phone.

'That's Shoreditch for you.' He says it's all changed in London. The crime wave has headed east and the centre has been taken over by more sophisticated crimes. What kind of crimes? I ask. Sid says there's things going on in central London that I walk past every day without any idea they're going on. Stealing phones is for kids. If I really want to see what the serious criminals are up to then he can show me. 'But you'll need to put on a shirt.'

Most Londoners will tell you that Covent Garden is for tourists. It's right at the centre of town and it's packed full of shops, bars, restaurants and theatres. The main square is where street performers, magicians and out-of-work actors perform al fresco shows for tips from the crowd. The market in the centre of the square is always bustling with groups of visitors from America, Asia and Europe. It feels a bit quaint. It's what, I imagine, most tourists think of when they think of the city.

It's certainly not Shoreditch.

Sid and I meet up in one of the old pubs along Drury Lane. It's a spit-and-sawdust boozer but the ale is some of the best in town. Sid says he wants to show me something. We round off our beers and I follow Sid along the trendy side streets to a club around the corner. It's a smart-looking London nightclub with a rope and doormen outside the door. The doormen are the size of orang-utans, not a neck between them. But they're nice as great-aunts to us. We're treated like a pair of lords, delicately escorted into the cloakroom area to pay the cover charge and then escorted downstairs to our seats in the bar.

Downstairs is a dark packed room with mirrored walls along three sides and a bar tucked away in the corner. The music is loud, blaring out transatlantic pop tunes. The clientele is exclusively men dressed in suits and women dressed in their underwear. Sid has taken me to a lap-dancing club.

I wonder what I'm doing here. I've never liked these places. And I've never really got the point of them either. What is it that some men enjoy about watching semi-naked women, who let's face it, they're never going to have sex with, dancing around for money? Sid says it's important for us to fit in so we have to each pick a girl and ask for a dance. He holds out his hand. I'm paying apparently. Thirty quid each.

Minutes later I'm sitting a dark corner while a woman dances around me in her underwear. Sid is sitting right next to me while another woman dances around him in her underwear. It's the least sexy thing I've ever experienced. I don't really know whether I'm supposed to be talking to her or to Sid. And if it's her then I've no idea what we're supposed to be talking about at all. It's hard to engage in small talk with a stranger who keeps trying to poke you in the eye with her boobs.

Then 'Melissa' and 'Jane' suggest we 'Go upstairs for some fun'. Sid nods and gives me the wink. This is it. He gets up to follow and we make our way through the club, up the stairs and into a larger room that has been divided up into private booths. The girls ask us to sit down. 'Would you like another drink?' asks Melissa or Jane. Sure. Why not? I feel like I might need it.

A waiter arrives with an ice bucket and some cheap champagne at almost the precise moment that Melissa or Jane takes her knickers off.

Whoa! I don't remember asking for either of those things to happen.

I'm starting to feel a little hemmed in. I start to ask Melissa or Jane about herself. She looks confused. I ask her where she's from. 'Ukraine,' she says.

And how did she end up working here.

'Why are you asking so many questions? You're freaking me out.'

I'm just trying to be friendly.

She looks around for something. I imagine maybe one of the heavies we saw at the door. And something tells me they won't be as nice this time. She seems to be able to tell that I'm not a typical customer and she's getting edgy. I nod to Sid. Think it's time to ask for the bill.

When the waiter comes back with the bill, I can't believe my eyes. It's nearly six hundred pounds! The cheap champagne comes in at over one hundred and fifty pounds and then another one hundred and fifty for each of the girls.

'I thought a dance was thirty pounds?' I ask.

'That's for downstairs,' says Melissa or Jane.

Upstairs there's an extra one hundred and twenty pounds to take her knickers off and a suggested gratuity of a hundred.

As soon as I start to show my displeasure at the bill, the big heavy guys, who I recognise from the door, arrive. One of them just points at the bill. Blank face. The implication is that this is non-negotiable so I reluctantly hand over my credit card. Once that's done, the guys lead us down towards the door. As we make our way back downstairs, Melissa or Jane is talking in Ukrainian with one of the guys. We've barely reached the main door when he shakes his finger at me. 'You don't come back here,' he says. 'No journalists here.' As if the six hundred pound bill hadn't put me off enough.

We've been clipped. This place is what is known in the trade as a clip joint because you come in flying and leave with your wings clipped. I've come across clip joints in Eastern Europe before but I'm shocked to see one still operating in the heart of London. I thought gentrification in this part of town had killed them all off long ago.

The heavy Ukrainian doormen ensure that people always pay and the girls act as honey traps to entice unsuspecting drunken men to buy into more than they bargained for. It's a simple scam but one that puts an expensive downer on the end of the night.

I'm about to wish Sid a good night when we're approached by a Nigerian guy. He just sidles up to us and very furtively whispers in my ear, 'You want the real thing?'

I look at Sid for a clue. Does he know what this is? Another twist in the scam perhaps? Sid looks blankly back with a shrug. He's in the dark too.

I ask the guy what he means. 'Real girls,' he says. 'For the real thing. Come.' He shuffles off towards a car parked across the street. Sid gives me a 'why not?' look and we bundle into the back seat of a beat-up Toyota Prius. No more than five minutes up the road, the Nigerian pulls up by a house near King's Cross. He gets out and gives us a big warm smile. 'Twenty pounds,' he says as we walk towards the door. I hand him a note, he knocks on the door and then he pats us both on the back.

Another girl in her underwear opens the door. 'Hello, gentlemen.' This is a very different environment to the one we were just in. There's a mish-mash of old chairs and sofas pushed around the edge of a tatty-looking room. In each seat there's a different woman sitting in her underwear.

These women are very different to the ones we saw at the club. These women are not tall and athletic with manicured nails and coiffured hair. These women are rather pasty and thin; some of them have bruises on their limbs. They're not confident and front-footed. They're quiet and hunted looking. There is no encouragement here for us to buy another bottle of champagne. Just waiting. Waiting for us to choose one of them. These women are not strippers. These women are prostitutes.

One of them starts chatting. She tells me that she's from London but that most of the others are 'foreigners'. I'm curious if they have any formal connection to the club. Is this another link in the chain? 'No,' she says. 'But we work together I suppose. They get them all worked up. And then we give them what they wanted in the first place.'

We apologise to the girls for wasting their time. Some kind of mistake. We make our excuses and leave. I say goodnight to Sid and take a taxi home. My girlfriend has invited friends back so the flat is full of drunken laughter and conversation when I come in. I say hello to everyone and then excuse myself so I can take a shower to freshen up. I'm undressing in the bedroom when it hits me. I just start to cry. I think about those girls sitting in their underwear in a damp crappy terraced house in King's Cross and I feel a profound sadness. Tonight's real victims are of course not the men who have blown hundreds of pounds at a London strip club before taking in a prostitute on the way home. They'll probably laugh about it on Monday and chalk it up as 'a good night out', as though it is somehow entertainment. The victims are the women I met at the end of the night – exploited, vulnerable and desperate. I've travelled all over the world and I've met pimps and prostitutes before, but it starts to sink in that tonight I came face to face with desperation just around the corner from where my life is happening, and that somehow makes me feel more sad.

A couple of days later I call Saul to ask if he's heard anything from the Indian phone thief. He confirms that it was him that stole my phone. He says the guy lives further east in Ilford but that he thinks he'll be a bit nervous about meeting me. Having said that, if I'm prepared to go to Ilford, then Saul says I can have the address.

I never got a good look at the guy who actually stole my phone but I can remember his friend clearly. He was around five foot five, square jaw and although his eyes were quite deep set, they had a sort of gentleness to them. He had a black Adidas cap pulled low over his forehead and he wore a silver bracelet on his right wrist. I'm pretty sure that I'd recognise him if I saw him again.

So I sit and wait on a street corner in Ilford. I sit where the road the thief lives on meets the high street.

I figure he has to walk past here to get into central London so even if I'm going to have to sit here all day, eventually I'm going to see him. I'm carefully scrutinising each person that walks by. Sure enough, not long after I arrive, I see him, or rather, I see them. The Indian guy has changed his clothes but he's still wearing the same black Adidas cap. And even though I didn't see his mate clearly, I'd bet a thousand pounds he's the other guy walking along the street.

I approach them immediately. They both look a little taken aback. 'All right mate?' I say to the Indian guy as friendly as I can. 'Remember me? We met in Hoxton Square.'

'No, man,' he says, shaking his head. 'I don't know who you are.'

I take a close look at him. Same gentle eyes. It is definitely the same guy.

'And you,' I point to the other guy. 'I thought you said you two didn't know each other?'

They look at each other. They look guilty. They look shifty. They're incredibly cautious. But I want them to take me to their boss. I'm more interested in who it is that they work for than I am in them, so I try to reassure them that everything is cool.

'I don't have your phone, man,' he says. 'I already sell it.'

'You already sold it?'

'Yeah, and I already spent the money, man.'

He starts to walk away down a side street. I'm happy to give up on the phone and forget about the money in exchange for some information. He's reluctant at first but after a few minutes he suggests we could go back to his house to talk. He says it's just around the corner. He introduces himself as Shaky.

Shaky's 'house' is a squat. The front door is boarded up with security panelling and there's graffiti painted across the walls. Shaky gives me an embarrassed shrug. 'No front door. We're jumping inside.' I follow him around the back of the small terrace house. He nimbly hops up onto the fence and then the flat roof before lifting himself up and in through the open first floor window. Are we breaking and entering? He chuckles as I crawl in through the window. I'm not sure he thought I'd actually follow. Before I have a chance to say anything, I get hit in the face by the most awful smell. The smell of human excrement.

The bedroom has a hole in the floorboards that drops down to the ground floor beneath. I cover my mouth and nose as I realise that the boys have been using this hole as a long drop toilet. There are fragments of toilet paper and a fog of flies beneath us. 'Come on,' Shaky says. 'We go next door.' I follow him into the other bedroom which has no furniture except for two stained mattresses on the floor. The window is smashed and the fragments of glass that cling on have been stained black with smoke. Shaky offers me a seat on the mattress next to him. I'm lost for words.

'Is this where you live?'

I already know the answer. Shaky lives in a two-bedroom squat where one of the bedrooms is literally a shit hole. I've been all over the world and I've seen extreme poverty but I have never seen anything as desperate as this. And we're in London not six miles from where I live.

Shaky asks me to wait while he prepares things. I'm not sure what he means until I realise that he and his friend are setting up some tin foil and a glass pipe. Shaky pulls two small plastic bags from his pocket containing drugs. They start smoking it right away.

'Heroin and crack,' says Shaky. 'All the money goes there.'

Shaky says he came to the UK from India in 2004 looking for work and got a job on a construction site. He was working illegally so the foreman would lock him and the other illegals in one of the site Portacabins each night. A couple of the other guys were heroin addicts and would smoke every night. Gradually Shaky got hooked too. Now he steals to feed his habit. And from the look of where he lives, he's not spending it on anything else.

'You know, lots of people are so drunk, it's easy to snatch phones.' He's exploiting someone else's vice to feed his own. 'With one phone, I can make one hundred and fifty pounds, which is ten bags. Five heroin and five crack.' And that's roughly what he and his mate smoke every day. 'We have to steal at least one phone every day,' he says. 'We smoke and then we go out and steal another one. Every day.'

While Shaky tells me his story, his friend racks up pipe after pipe. They chase the heroin down the foil and then smoke another crack pipe. All the time they take turns until an hour later four bags are gone. I wonder who else they work with. 'No one, man.' He shakes his head. 'Only us.'

These guys are a two-man crime wave. A couple of phones every day to pay for their astronomical drug habit. They exist outside of any gang and they answer only to themselves. Shaky says this is how it is for other thieves they know too. It's all about drugs and their addiction to it. It's so terribly sad. I came looking for a sophisticated criminal network but all I've uncovered is a couple of addicts eking out a pathetic existence in a shit-infested squat. It's a million miles away from the London I thought I knew.

I say goodbye to Shaky and his friend. 'Sorry for the trouble I caused you, man,' he says, shaking my hand. 'It's my problem.'

I climb back out of the window and down to the street below. I leave Ilford and head back west towards the centre of town. I think about Shaky and the girls in King's Cross and I feel humbled by what I've seen. I thought I knew this city. But like many, I have been seduced by the bright lights and the razzmatazz and been blinded to the crime that is fuelled by poverty and addiction. I have travelled the world under the misapprehension that London was somehow better off than other places, when in actual fact, I have witnessed destitution here more profound than anywhere else.

The gangs of East London were once world-renowned. The Krays and the Hoxton Mob fought turf wars over spheres of influence and their leaders were photographed with young starlets hanging off their arms. They're still the subject of movies. But those days would seem to be well and truly gone. London has outsourced its crime. Ukrainian heavies run strippers, while Nigerian taxi drivers double up as pimps and Indian drug addicts steal phones. London. A city so truly international, that even the criminals now come from far and wide.

EPILOGUE

CRIME PAYS. AND we're the suckers that pay for it. We're the fools who don't check the change, the idiots who leave drinks unattended, the schmucks who put wallets in our back pockets, the careless drunks who get into unlicensed taxis late at night. It's our fault. We're to blame. If it wasn't for us then there wouldn't be any crime.

This is a compelling narrative for both criminal and victim to adhere to. For the criminal it helps absolve responsibility. They are all at fault, says the criminal, so it's society's problem. For the victim too it is comforting to think like this. It's easier to pick up and carry on because we are empowered by the belief that it won't happen again if we do things differently next time. There won't be a next time if we're more careful.

So are the criminals that different from their victims? Aren't they just practising what the rest of us preach? Crime is an industry in which competition and survival of the fittest plays out like any other. As long as capitalism produces inequality then there will be poor people stealing and rich people from whom to steal, won't there? As many of the criminals I met said to me: isn't crime just a business like anything else?

To write this book I had to get close to the criminals and to do that, I often had to reserve judgement of them. But maybe it is now time to consider them less dispassionately.

Crime is indeed a huge industrial-like sector of the global economy. Compare it for a moment to healthcare. Just as there are doctors and nurses and pharmacists so there are thieves and forgers and kidnappers. They've all become specialists in their fields by developing and honing particular skill sets over time until they become the very best at what they do. They have families and mortgages and they need to earn money to service them. But deep down they are not the same.

The people working in healthcare are generally driven vocationally to help others. They earn money in a way which, at the same time, makes a contribution to the society in which they live. Sure, healthcare industries the world over are imperfect and there's bad apples in every barrel, but on the whole, there is an approximate equilibrium between the contribution these individuals make and the remuneration that they receive.

But the criminal economy has no such equilibrium. Crime takes from society with both hands. And that is nobody's fault but the criminals themselves. That is on them.

I began this book wondering if the real life criminal was very different from the one of the silver screen and I naturally had preconceptions about what criminals would really be like if I met them. I saw criminals as mysterious, complex rogues, not because I knew any personally but because I'd seen them on TV. In TV shows like *The Sopranos* and *Breaking Bad* the criminals are portrayed as dark and dangerous but they also possess a sensitive human side that feels pain and even remorse; they're complex, engaging characters.

I was surprised to find so many of the criminals I met were in real life also so likeable. On a superficial level there were several that I felt I could happily hang out with for an afternoon. Michael, the Three-Card Monte specialist, for example, is a man who's led an incredible life; a life spent running from war across the continent, surviving on his wits and his skills. He's a superb raconteur, at least until the seventeenth beer kicks in, funny, unpredictable and, while not the kind of person you'd necessarily ask to Sunday lunch with your mum, still great company for an hour or two.

But then I look again at the victims and I remind myself that these criminals are bad people. Bad, predatory people in fact. Rotten to the core. I'd never want to spend another minute with the torturer I met in Bogotá or the 'rehabilitated' murderer who steals cannabis in Birmingham. These are men who think it's okay to cause people physical pain and potentially life-changing psychological trauma because they're in need of money.

I began to re-evaluate these individuals and I wondered what they had in common. I listed out the common personality traits that they shared and it began to remind me of something. In Jon Ronson's *The Psychopath Test*, he describes how psychologists use the PCL-R, also known as the psychopathy checklist, to evaluate psychopathy. I read it through and it sent a chill down my spine. I found myself asking to what extent the criminals I met might be psychopaths. Psychopathy is generally described as someone who exhibits certain characteristics, the most common of which are:

- glib and superficial charm
- grandiose sense of self worth
- pathological lying
- cunning and manipulativeness
- lack of remorse or guilt
- superficial emotional responsiveness
- callousness and lack of empathy.

Looking at this list, I start to realise how many of the characters in this book could be described in these terms.

I begin to see Michael's charm as superficial. Then I remember Danny's cast-iron grandiose self-belief that he was a modern-day Robin Hood. I think about the

Mumbai casting director Molly's pathological pack of lies about photo shoots and Equity cards. I baulk at the memory of Crystal's cunning and manipulation as she lured me into a backroom Razzle game. I compare how little remorse or guilt Cam showed when he described torturing his victims with his sun bed. Not to mention the superficial emotional response of the Counterfeit Gang as they laughed about shooting a cop in the head. But it is the last thing on the list that gives me goosebumps.

In nearly every case, the criminals I met displayed a callous lack of empathy.

Maybe that lack of empathy is necessary to be a successful criminal. So many of them, from the guys who stand in front of victims and charm them out of cash, to the guys who drug and torture victims, are causing harm to innocent people and shrugging it off as 'just business'. But kidnapping someone off the street, holding them at gunpoint for an hour while you steal five hundred dollars from their ATM is not 'just business'. It is all too clear that many of these people only see the five hundred dollars and conveniently ignore that their victim will be irrevocably damaged.

I whimsically wondered when I started this journey if I would find my own 'criminal identity'. I dreamed that there might be a criminal career out there that might suit me. It's a question that I asked myself again while writing this book: what if I were to become a criminal? If

I could put my morality to one side. If I could deal with the paranoia of always looking over my shoulder and accept the likelihood that I'd spend some time behind bars. What kind of criminal would I be? What kind of criminal could I be?

The truth is that I could not be a criminal. I'm not cut out for it. Sure I found some of it thrilling. I'll admit that the act of running with the gang was momentarily exhilarating but the bottom line is that I couldn't sleep at night if I knew I had hurt others. I can't sideline my morality. I couldn't handle the fear of being caught. I'm simply too sensitive and fearful to live that life.

I think about how Danny explained why he thought I could never be a pickpocket. He didn't say 'Because you're not a psychopath' but rather he explained it in terms of fear. Danny admits freely that he doesn't experience fear the same way that I do. The brain of a psychopath doesn't react with fear the same way as yours or mine. In tests on criminal psychopaths, researchers have found that they lack the fear conditioning that causes the rest of us to be afraid when we know something bad is coming. They used an experiment that involves them playing a certain tune before administering an electric shock. You and I would learn that the tune means there is a shock coming and modify our behaviour accordingly but psychopaths' brains don't show the same changes when the song plays. This lack of anxiety over the future and the consequences of their actions is what Danny was talking about.

All of the criminals in this book might do bad things but they're certainly not all psychopaths. Shaky, the London phone thief, is an addict; Mariella, who tried to seduce me in Bogotá, seemed genuinely vulnerable and emotional when confronted, and the fake tour guide in Mumbai, as well as the smugglers and fake artefact sellers in Jerusalem, probably fall outside of the description too. Also the Artist, despite the fact that he couldn't stop running those printing presses, did show some signs of remorse when he heard that his actions had indirectly led to the death of a young girl.

But the others?

Nawlins Crystal, Cannabis Cam, the Counterfeit Gang, the pickpockets Danny and Chris, Three-Card Monte Michael, Johnny the Pimp, Fernando the Bogotá torturer, the Mexican kidnapper and Mumbai's Fake Cop are all on the psychopath spectrum. They are all gods of their own worlds, heroes of their own narratives. They lack empathy or remorse. Every one of them callously manipulates their victims with their superficial charms. They fall into the category of 'deranged' rather than 'desperate'.

Danny is typical. He would like you to see him as Robin Hood. But he is nothing of the sort. Danny is a bully and a misogynist. Sure, he has the charm and the looks to make it as a thief in a town where thievery is everywhere, but like the actors in the movies, that's all for show. He couldn't care a damn about how any of his victims feel.

Many people rightly believe that people become criminals because of wider issues. Where you live, family background and job opportunities are all-important factors in determining crime hotspots. Shaky, the drug addict phone thief, would fall into this category. Who knows if he would have become a criminal but for the circumstances that led to his addiction?

But by this theory everyone who is in work and content with life wouldn't commit crime. And I'm not sure that is true of the criminals I met, many of whom seemed to genuinely enjoy what they do.

I wonder if this feeds into why particular criminals do particular crimes. Why is Danny a pickpocket and not a forger? Why is Johnny a pimp and not a Three-Card Monte conman? I think this comes down to talent and environment.

First, Danny is young, confident and particularly dextrous. He plays to his strengths when he chooses to become a pickpocket. Like the rest of us, he chooses his career rationally by working out what he is good at and pursuing that path. Maybe he never became a forger because he wasn't very good at art when he was younger. Or he doesn't have the patience to sit down and painstakingly set the printing plates necessary so that the design is perfect, as Hector does. Or maybe it's because the environment wasn't right.

Danny lives in Barcelona and not Buenos Aires. Spain's lax laws with regard to petty thievery make for the perfect place to be a pickpocket but there isn't the cultural history of currency forgery that there is in Argentina to encourage him to be a counterfeiter. He can only adapt to the circumstances in which he finds himself.

Seen this way, what emerges is a pattern of criminality around the globe where skills are matched to opportunity in the same way as in other legitimate areas of the job market. It's what economists refer to as Matching Theory. Criminals adjust to fit the environment in which they find themselves and the skills follow, in which case the environment becomes the driving force.

Certainly there are cultural patterns that emerge. It's no surprise that in cultures like the USA and Latin America where guns are prevalent, the criminals tend to use guns. I had a pistol pointed at me three times: once in Argentina and twice in the US. Also, the way criminals worked with others seemed very influenced by how developed the city was. In wealthier cities like London, Barcelona and New Orleans, where law enforcement is perhaps better funded, crime seemed more opportunistic and less coordinated than in poorer cities like Mexico

City and Buenos Aires where individuals were operating within loosely organised criminal networks.

I ask myself whether perhaps this might be down to how politics shape the crime that will plague the electorate. In cities where more money is dedicated to fighting crime, the criminal is forced to turn opportunist. Here the most desperate, the junkies, have no choice but to hustle and steal and engage in the pettiest of crimes. Look then at Jerusalem, a dysfunctional political system that has both fuelled the fires of rebellion that gave rise to the Arab Spring and provided the perfect market place for those selfishly profiting from it. And in Latin America, where law enforcement is so corrupt as to render it ineffective, the criminals have the power to organise themselves into gangs and raise the stakes considerably for their victims.

But irrespective of these environmental factors, the choice to pursue a life of crime comes back to the individual. It is individuals who weigh up the pros and cons and it is individuals who make the choice as to whether or not to commit crime. This is why some people who come from poor areas become criminals while others do not.

When I think about how the people who have chosen a life of crime stack up against those who have stayed on the right side of the law, I wonder if improving social conditions would have any effect. With more opportunity, the genuine psychopaths would still be bad people, they'd just be doing something else. Much has already been written about the prevalence of psychopaths in high-ranking positions in politics and commerce.

In the meantime what do we do? Because being the victim of a crime is awful and criminals are everywhere. It's all right to admit that. Don't make it your fault because it isn't your fault.

We need to protect ourselves from crime. We must look out for ourselves. And that means being able to spot the criminals.

To do that it is first important to remember that they need us. And what's more, they need us to act in certain ways for them to thrive. The expansion of global tourism in the last fifty years has facilitated the growth of the crime industry. Tourists are great victims and criminals actively seek them out. Off-guard and not knowing the rules puts you at the greatest risk and so when you're travelling you need to be extra vigilant.

Simple rules can be followed to reduce your chances of being a victim of crime when you're away from home:

- never leave a wallet/passport in a back pocket
- never leave the zips on your backpack in the middle, do them all the way to one side
- never drape a bag or coat over the back of a chair while you eat al fresco

- never leave your drink unattended, or if you have done, buy a fresh one
- avoid going to the ATM after dark and never between 11 p.m. and midnight
- never get into a taxi at night without first checking the driver's ID matches his licence
- never play illegal gambling games either on the street or off it
- never leave your phone on the table of the cafe or bar
- avoid buying expensive souvenirs unless you know your stuff
- if you want to be a movie star then get an agent.

And remember too that you're still susceptible at home as well as abroad. After all, Cam operates his evil torture trade a couple of miles from where my mother lives and Shaky is stealing phones in a neighbourhood close to my own house.

What do those two have in common? Drugs. Of course most people who use illegal drugs are non-problematic users and don't have to commit crimes to pay for them. But many of the three hundred thousand regular heroin and crack users in the UK do turn to crime to get money. That's a lot of theft if they're funding thirty-thousand-pounds-a-year habits like Shaky is. And then there's the five hundred thousand people growing cannabis in the

UK who are targets for Cam and his ilk. As Cam says, it would put him out of business if it was legalised.

Decriminalisation of drugs is one of the things governments can look at to help make us safer from the criminals. There are others. Why on earth are the laws regarding theft so relaxed in Spain? This is clearly something for their government to look at if thieves from around the world are queuing up to get into the country. It's also high time that Argentina's government looked at how it can make its currency more secure. And the whole international community needs to take action now to stop the systematic pillaging of the Middle East's cultural heritage before it is lost for ever.

But however we try to reduce crime, we'll never rid ourselves completely of the criminals. Maybe we need to have them in real life so we can write them into our fictional stories. Certainly the world would be a less interesting place without them. In the real world we can take some comfort from the fact that there are more of us than there are of them. On dry land, we have the sharks outnumbered. Just be careful when you go in the water.

ACKNOWLEDGEMENTS

FIRSTLY I'D LIKE to thank everyone who appears in the book. A bunch of rogues and scoundrels they may be, but without their willingness and openness I would have had nothing to write about. I was constantly amazed at how people who operated on the wrong side of the law could be persuaded to converse so openly about their activities. Maybe I have their psychopathy to thank for that too!

I'd also like to thank all the fantastic producers and crew that I worked with on various films for TV. They're too numerous to list here (you know who you are) but I would like to make special mention of Peter and Brent and André who I shared many an hour discussing bad guys with. Also Martin, Van, Steeve, Carl, Marta, George, Roz, Mike and Paul who travelled many a mile with me on the road. I couldn't have written this book without your help. Thank you all.

I am also indebted to my publisher Hannah MacDonald at September Publishing for her insightful edits and consistent support along the way to this final draft, as well as all her team at September, including Justine and Charlotte. And a big thank you to my agent

Gordon Wise for pushing it under Hannah's nose in the first place. I've so enjoyed the collaboration with you all and have felt very safe and supported since day one.

A big thank you also to my draft-readers, Mum and Paddy. Between you I think I have the demographic covered. Your feedback and insights were incredibly helpful in the later stages as I tried to work out what this book was really about.

But the biggest thank you I save for the woman that met me halfway through this adventure and didn't run a mile. In chapter one she was but a glint in the eye, but by the end she was my wife. To Phoebe Waller-Bridge for listening and supporting and reading and discussing and all the other things you do for me every day. Thank you.

ABOUT THE AUTHOR

Conor Woodman has been a producer and presenter in factual television for many years. His series include *Scam City, Around the World in 80 Trades, Watchdog* and, most recently, *Hunting Nazi Treasure*. He has written two previous books, *The Adventure Capitalist* and *Unfair Trade*, which was long listed for the Orwell prize. *True Appaloosa*, his first feature length documentary film, premiered at the Sun Valley Film Festival in 2015 and aired on BBC4 as *The Secret Horse* to wide critical acclaim.

www.conorwoodman.com